It's a
Jesus
Thing

THE BOOK FOR
WANNA BE-LIEVERS

Scott Kelby
The author of a bunch of best-selling "non-Jesusy" books

It's a Jesus Thing

The "It's a Jesus Thing" Book Team

CONTRIBUTING AUTHORS
Dave Gales
Douglas Poole

CONTRIBUTING EDITOR
Dave Moser

EDITOR
Kim Doty

E-BOOK PRODUCTION
Dave Korman

COVER DESIGN
Scott Kelby
Jessica Maldonado

COVER IMAGE
iStockphoto/Peter Booth

PUBLISHED BY
Kelby Publishing

Copyright © 2012 Scott Kelby

Composed in the fonts Myriad, Lucida Grande, and Helvetica.

ISBN 13: 978-1-937038-17-5
ISBN 10:   1-937038-17-5

9 8 7 6 5 4 3 2 1

Printed and bound in the United States of America

www.scottkelby.com

To my dear friend and mentor Dave Gales,
who gave me my first Bible and
changed my life forever. I couldn't have
written this book without you.

Acknowledgments

After writing books for 13 years now, I still find that the thing that's the hardest for me to write in any book is writing the acknowledgments. It also, hands down, takes me longer than any other pages in the book. For me, I think the reason I take these acknowledgments so seriously is because it's the only time I really put down on paper how truly grateful I am to be surrounded by such great friends and a family that truly makes my life a joy. I also know why it takes so long—you type a lot slower with tears in your eyes.

To my remarkable wife, Kalebra: We've been married 22 years now, and you still continue to amaze me and everyone around you. I've never met anyone more compassionate, more loving, more hilarious, and more genuinely beautiful, and I'm so blessed to be going through life with you, to have you as the mother of my children, my business partner, my private pilot, Chinese translator, gourmet chef, personal artist, and best friend. You truly are the type of woman love songs are written for and, as anyone who knows me will tell you, I am, without a doubt, the luckiest man alive to have you for my wife.

To my son, Jordan: It's every dad's dream to have a relationship with his son like I have with you, and I'm so proud of the bright, caring, creative young man you've become. I can't wait to see the amazing things life has in store for you, and I just want you to know that watching you grow into the person you are is one of my life's greatest joys.

To my precious little girl, Kira: You have been blessed in a very special way, because you are a little clone of your mom, which is the most wonderful thing I could have possibly wished for you. I see all her gifts reflected in your eyes, and though you're still too young to have any idea how blessed you are to have Kalebra as your mom, one day—just like Jordan—you will.

To my big brother, Jeff: You have always been, and will always be, a hero to me. So much of who I am, and where I am, is because of your influence, guidance, caring, and love as I was growing up. Thank you for teaching me to always take the high road, for always knowing the right thing to say at the right time, and for having so much of our dad in you. I wrote this book for you, and my greatest wish is that it works.

There are three people without whom this book would have never been written:

To Dave Gales: This book is dedicated to you, because I never would have even attempted to write this book, if I didn't' know you, and didn't know with every bone in my body that you would want to help. Because of your humility, you would never imagine the impact that you've had on those around you, and perhaps that's what makes you even more special. This book has your fingerprints, your words, your ideas, and your feedback all over it, and it's a far better book because of your involvement. Thank you, Dave. You continue to bless me and those around you.

To Douglas Poole: You've always been a gifted pastor and a caring friend, but by being willing to help me every step of the way through this book, you also showed an incredible amount of courage. You know more than anyone the slings and arrows that I'll face for writing this, and as the man who sat with me for countless hours, letting me pick your brain, helping me break through walls, and teaching me more about God than I ever thought I'd know (to create a book that we both know was way over my head), you took a much greater risk than I, yet you never blinked. You're so committed to helping others find God, and to live a life full of meaning and purpose, that you were willing to step way, way outside the box and help a friend who could not have done this without you. This book would not be what it is were it not for your help, ideas, and backbone. I owe you an awful lot, my friend.

To Dave Moser: The third piece of this puzzle, and my dear friend for many years, who pushed me to write this book, who researched and uncovered key concepts included in this book, and who gave himself selflessly to make certain that this book saw the light of day. Your commitment to this project has left me humbled, and your caring and encouragement helped me to get through it in one piece. Your faith in this book and how it needed to be written never wavered, and that helped me in ways you'll never know. It was because you believed that I could do it, that I did it. We did it!

My heartfelt thanks to my "beta" testers: Pastor William Rice, Rev. John A. D'Antonio, and Rev. Daniel Francis, C.Ss.R., whose input, suggestions, and expertise made this book significantly better than it would have been. I'm tremendously grateful to have had such remarkable men of faith help shape and mold this project.

To Kim Doty: You've been editing my computer books for years now, and when I told you about this project, you couldn't have volunteered faster to be the editor, which is all I could have asked for. This is the most important book I've ever written, and it's truly an honor (and a very big win for us all) to have you as the book's editor.

To Kathy Siler: I owe a huge debt of gratitude to my Executive Assistant and chief Wonder Woman, Kathy Siler, who runs a whole side of my business life, and skillfully balanced a lot of plates in the air to give me the time I needed to write this book. Thank you, thank you, thank you. It means more than you know.

To Brad Moore and Bill Fortney: My thanks to you both for lending me your wonderful images for the book. It's an honor having such awesome photographers represented in the book. You guys rock!

Thanks to my mentors, whose wisdom and whip-cracking have helped me immeasurably throughout my life, including John Graden, Jack Lee, Dave Gales, Judy Farmer, and Douglas Poole.

Thanks to people like **Molly Bail, David Dwyer, and Jean A. Kendra** who have inspired me through their giving hearts and willingness to help others less fortunate, no matter what it takes.

In the 50+ books I've written, I always end my acknowledgments the same way— by thanking **God and His Son Jesus Christ** for leading me to the woman of my dreams, for blessing us with two amazing children, for allowing me to make a living doing something I truly love, for always being there when I need Him, for blessing me with a wonderful, fulfilling, and happy life, and such a warm, loving family to share it with. This one's for You.

About the Author

Scott Kelby

Scott is a photographer, designer, and award-winning author of more than 50 books on technology and digital imaging (including books on everything from the iPhone to Adobe Photoshop). His book, *The Digital Photography Book,* vol. 1 is the best-selling book in history on digital photography.

For six years straight, Scott was awarded the distinction of being the world's #1 best-selling author of all technology books, and he was recently named the #1 best-selling author of all photography books. His books have been translated into dozens of different languages, including Russian, Chinese, French, German, Spanish, Korean, Polish, Greek, Turkish, Japanese, Dutch, and Taiwanese, among others.

Scott is Editor-in-Chief and Publisher of *Photoshop User* magazine, and is host of the weekly videocast about the photography industry, *The Grid*. He is President and co-founder of the National Association of Photoshop Professionals (NAPP), the trade association for Adobe® Photoshop® users, and is President of the software, education, and publishing firm Kelby Media Group.

Scott is Training Director for the Adobe Photoshop Seminar Tour, Conference Technical Chair for the Photoshop World Conference & Expo, and is a speaker at trade shows and events around the world. For more information on Scott, visit his daily blog at www.scottkelby.com.

Contributing Authors

Dave Gales
Dave's passion is helping people. After pastoring for 20 years, he served as an international relief worker and had the opportunity to deliver medical supplies to churches in Cuba, distribute rice in Indonesia after a devastating earthquake and tsunami, and to deliver donated items to the Gulf Coast region after Hurricane Katrina. He is currently a member of the Kelby Training Live team that conducts one-day Photoshop seminars in cities across the United States, Canada, and Europe.

Douglas Poole
Douglas is the Senior Pastor of Cypress Meadows Community Church in Clearwater, Fl. He has a B.A. in Bible and Theology from Crown College in Minnesota and a Master of Divinity degree from Asbury Theological Seminary in Kentucky. He is passionate about the local church and sailing. And crazy about his wife Jacqueline, their four kids, and their grandchildren.

Table of Contents

Table of Contents

I Had No Intentions of Writing This Book

It's 8:25 a.m. one morning, I just dropped my son off at middle school, and now I'm heading to the office. I've got a good 20 minutes before I actually make it there, and on the way I drive by this little run-down golf course where my older brother Jeff and I played a round a few years back. I could picture my brother and I heading for cover when it started raining about four holes in.

So, now I'm thinking about my big brother, who is, by the way, the best brother a guy could ever have. But, he's not just a great brother, he's really a great person all around—always has been. He's one of the most generous, kind, thoughtful, honest, genuine, giving, loving guys, who's not going to heaven, that you'd ever want to meet.

And as I'm driving, I just can't understand how someone who has always been such a good guy, and has helped as many people as he has, has stopped just short of securing his place in heaven. He does all the "right" things, he's extremely ethical, moral, and compassionate and he does everything you'd imagine a faithful Christian would do each day, except for just one thing: he doesn't believe in Jesus. He's stopped just short of "sealing the deal." He's *this* close. *This* close!

He's kind of like someone who has been working on getting their private pilot's license for a while and is already doing their solo flights. They go out to the airfield, they pre-flight the plane, talk to the tower, take off into the sky, and bring the plane back in for a safe landing—all by themselves. They're doing everything a pilot does, but they're just short of actually being a real licensed pilot. They still need that one thing (a check ride with an FAA examiner) that takes them from a student going through the motions to licensed pilot. They're so close. They're *this* close. Yet, sadly, statistics show that most student pilots never take that final step.

And that's my brother. He's not trying to be a pilot of course, but he does all these things that sound like someone who's living their life as a Christian would do, but he's stopped just short of accepting Christ and sealing the deal. I know people who have earned their pilot's license (my wife, for example), and let me tell you, the test is much harder than the one for becoming a Christian (especially since there is no test). My brother's missing one thing: faith. He just won't take that last step that transforms him from a nice guy to a forgiven guy who is one day going to heaven. I just can't understand it, and for some reason this particular morning it's really getting to me.

But, it's not just my brother, it's a number of great people I really care about, like my buddy Marvin, who is a physician who genuinely cares for his patients. He has dedicated his life not just to helping his patients, but to training other physicians on how to be a compassionate, empathetic doctor, and how to communicate with people with terminal diseases to treat more than just their medical symptoms—to treat the whole person. He's a remarkable man, who lives a remarkable life, and does lots of amazing things each day, except he keeps missing one crucial thing that could transform his life forever. He'd be the first one to tell you there's something missing in his life—a hole within that nothing's been able to fill.

I could go on and on, because sadly I know a lot of people like this. So, I'm driving to work and thinking of all these people in my life, and while I'm frustrated that they're stopping short of having a real relationship with God, I'm even more frustrated in myself because I'm so bad at telling them face-to-face about God and His Son Jesus. Anytime I've tried, I've become incredibly uncomfortable. I think part of it is that I never saw myself as one of those annoying "Have you heard how the Lord has changed my life?" people. So much so, that anytime I talk about it, I'm literally squirming. Talking one-on-one like that about God is clearly a talent I don't have, which is made worse by the fact that I make a part of my living giving live workshops and presentations. Arrrgghhh!!!

I'm halfway there

So, now I'm about half way to work, and I'm thinking that I'm really letting these people down, and I'm thinking to myself, "I wish there was a book or something that I could give them that would answer their questions, and show them that they wouldn't be giving up anything—they'd be gaining everything!" Something short and sweet, that's in plain English, and not too "religiousy," and it can't be the standard "come to Jesus" book that just quotes the Bible. In fact, I wish there was a book that didn't quote the Bible at all that I could give them.

Now I'm thinking, "I wish there was a book about becoming a Christian that's like my book, *The Digital Photography Book.*" That book has become the best-selling book on digital photography in history, and people have told me that what they love about it is the fact that I left out all the technical stuff. Instead, I just showed them which buttons to push, which tricks to use, and just a bunch of straight-to-the-point stuff about how to get better photos. Now I need a book just like that, but about Jesus, to give to my brother and my friends. It's got to be simple, clear, and right to the point, without all the religious speak that messes up every other book that I've ever considered buying for them.

So, I'm still driving and thinking, "Man, I wish there was a book like that…" and then it hit me. Oh no! I'm supposed to write that book. I didn't hear a voice, or see a vision, or anything like that, but I just knew right then, in my heart, I was supposed to write that book.

I was going to need some help

Once I realized that I had to write this book, I got kind of freaked out because as I mentioned earlier, I'm uncomfortable with evangelizing the whole "Jesus thing" in person. But as I thought about it, I realized that a lot of people surrounding me are really great at it. Like my good friend Dave Gales, to whom this book is dedicated. Dave was the pastor of the first church I attended as an adult, and Dave is, hands down, the best plain-English speaker I've ever heard on the topic. I knew Dave would be a huge help to me (plus, he is an expert and he lives for this stuff).

Then, there's the pastor at my current church, Douglas Poole—he's been at our small local church for 30+ years now. He started this church straight out of pastor college (they call it seminary), and he's a wealth of knowledge on God, and a fantastic communicator who has taught me a lot. There are also my Christian friends at work, and in our industry, and people I deal with every day who all bring something different to the table about God. And, there's my buddy, Dave Moser—one the best guys on the planet, a dedicated, educated Christian, and a guy with volumes of experience in the book publishing business. I knew when I told him about it, he'd make absolutely certain this book would get published.

Plus, I've got people like my brother Jeff—he'd be a great testing ground. So would Marvin. And and I have a lot of other friends that I'd love to give a book like this to, and I'd get their feedback and deal with their questions and challenges before the book was even published.

And, although I'm really bad at the face-to-face "Jesus thing," at least I can write. I've written more than 50 books now on everything from how to use an iPhone to Adobe Photoshop to photography, but I've never written, or even had the inkling to write anything like this before. But, for whatever reason, I was supposed to write this book, so I developed it the same way I had done with my book, *The Digital Photography Book*.

Why I wanted to do this

I worry about my friends and my brother and I truly want them to experience genuine happiness, a sense of purpose, and meaning in their lives (plus, I don't want any of them to go to "the hot place"). I want the great things happening inside of me to happen inside of them. I want them, and you, to finally "get" what Jesus is all about. Now, if you're thinking, "Oh yeah, Scott. Right. You care about me." Yes. I do. And if the idea of caring about people you've never met seems disingenuous or hokey to you, then man—you really need this book.

You can't just flip a switch

Although the act of becoming a Christian is amazingly easy, getting to the point where you sincerely believe and are ready to take that step usually takes some time. It's not like flipping a switch, it's a process—like learning to cook. At first, you're kind of skeptical about your cooking skills ("Can I really become a great cook?"). But then you learn a few basics, and some more things, and you get some of your cooking questions answered, and soon you start to realize there's a chef inside you after all. Then the day comes when you feel like you really know what you're doing, and you cook your friends or family a really amazing meal. You are a chef! It doesn't happen on day one. It takes a little time. Some people pick up cooking really fast, others take longer, but as Chef Gusteau says, "Anyone can cook." So, in a way, you're holding a cookbook of sorts in your hands, and my hope for this book is that it guides you along your path. That it helps you learn the basics and answers some of your lingering questions, relieves some of your worries, and breaks down some negative stereotypes and myths. I hope it leads you down a path that truly gives you enough confidence and faith to know there's more to life than you're living, and that it gives you what you need to take that one extra step that changes everything.

I knew this wouldn't be easy

When I wrote *The Digital Photography Book*, I first looked at all the other books out there on digital photography, and I looked at why they weren't connecting with readers. Then, I set out to reinvent how digital photography books were written. I wanted to use that same type of thinking here in *It's a Jesus Thing*. I had to break the mold and do something really different, even if it went against what Christian experts believe is the "right" way to write this type of book. I needed to write a book that would convince my brother, and Marvin, and my other friends "on the edge," and every other great person out there just like them that they can finally find that one thing that's missing in their lives. The one thing that would change everything for them here in this life, and after. So, I had my work cut out for me. I knew this wouldn't be easy (and it wasn't. This book, nearly my shortest ever, took me five times longer to write than any other I've written).

Things happen for a reason

Now, maybe it's all just one big happy coincidence that all these things and all these people just happened to come together perfectly, right now, in my life for me to be able to write this book, but I don't think that's the case. I think this book was supposed to happen. I think maybe that's why God gave me the ability to write books in the first place (which is somewhat a miracle in itself, considering I have no formal training in writing whatsoever and hated writing and English in school) and why He got me back into photography (even though I have no formal photography training, either). I think it's why I became such great friends with Dave Gales and Douglas Poole, and even Marvin. Plus, I think my brother really needs me to write this book (even if he doesn't know it yet).

I don't think any of this was just dumb luck. I think it's part of a bigger plan, and I don't think it's just a coincidence that you're holding this book right now. In fact, maybe you are the very person I was supposed to write it for. Let's find out.

Nine Things You'll Want to Know...

SCOTT KELBY

(1) I'm figuring that you already believe in God. Surveys show that 97% of Americans already believe in God, so it's almost a lock that you do, too. I also imagine if you're reading this book, somebody bought it for you (and I don't think anyone would buy you a book about Jesus, if you didn't at least kinda believe in God in the first place), and that's actually pretty cool because that means that somebody cares enough about you that they spent their hard-earned money to buy you a book they think will help you in your life. So, I'm going on the assumption that you at least kinda believe in God (that's a good thing, because if you don't, then it makes the rest of this book, about His Son Jesus and becoming a Christian, a really tough sell. By the way, on the off-chance you're in that 3% that doesn't believe in God, I wrote two extra chapters just for you at www.wannabelievers.com /thegodthing). And, just so you know, right up front, here's what I'm trying to do with this book: I want to show you how taking the simple step of becoming a Christian is going to give your life real meaning, and make you a much more fulfilled and generally happier person all around (which I truly believe it will, for a whole bunch of reasons that I go into throughout the book). But if you just cringed at the thought of becoming "one of those Christians," then the first chapter is just for you, because it takes you through all those stereotypes and myths you've probably heard over the years, and after reading that chapter you'll be able to breath a sigh of relief.

(2) This book is not for Christians. If you're already a Christian, this book is totally not for you on any level. In fact, all this book will do for you is make you really, really mad, because I purposely didn't follow all the tried and true rules for writing books about becoming a Christian. For example, I don't reference Scripture. At all. Now, if you're wondering, "What is Scripture?" then this book actually *is* for you. However, if you just screamed, "What!?! You don't reference Scripture!?!" then I'm begging

Before Reading This Book!

you—put the book down and just walk away. Here's why I did it: quoting the Bible for people who don't already believe in the Bible would be like saying, "Ya know that book you don't believe in? Well, here's what it says to do." So, I made a conscience decision to break the mold and not to go that route. Now, I fully expect to catch loads of heat for this from "serious Christians," but I'm okay with that because when I last checked on Amazon.com alone, there were more than 257,000 books on Christianity that do quote Scripture, so it's not like this one book will make them miss their quota.

(3) I don't use "religious speak." I'm just a regular guy (I didn't go to Bible college, or study in Rome, etc.) and since I don't use religious terms in my day-to-day life, I don't use them here in the book either. I talk to you just like I'm talking to a friend, so the book is very casual and right to the point.

(4) This book isn't about picking a particular denomination. I'm not representing Catholics, or Baptists, or Presbyterians, or any other particular Christian denomination, so just know up front that I'm not trying to secretly lead you toward one or the other. My job ends at getting you to finally "get" Jesus—in helping you fill that missing gap in your life—and if you do choose a particular denomination, my hope is that you find one that's a perfect fit for you. If you don't pick one at all, that's not a deal breaker either.

(5) There are lots of pretty pictures. I'm a photographer, so I've included some of my photography in the book, plus I asked two of my friends (Bill Fortney and Brad Moore), who are famous photographers in their own right, if they would lend me some of their favorite images for the book. They're pictures of beautiful places (from Bill and me) and cool concert shots (from Brad). I hope you like 'em.

Here Are the Other Four

(6) All the profits from this book go to maintaining the Springs of Hope Kenya orphanage.
Last year, an amazing husband and wife team from our hometown sold their house, their cars—everything—and moved to Kenya (with their teenage son) to try and build an orphanage from scratch. With help from donations, some contributed by people who read my daily blog, here it is a year or so later and the orphanage is up and running and caring for some really wonderful kids. However, feeding, clothing, and educating these kids is an ongoing need, which is why 100% of the profits from this book will go to the Springs of Hope Kenya orphanage charity. If they wind up getting enough money so it's not a daily issue, I'll find another charity that needs it as badly as they need it right now.

(7) I had to choose one name for priest/pastor/deacon/minister/bishop, etc. In the book, when I mention the person that leads a church service, like a priest/pastor/deacon/minister/bishop, etc., it would probably drive you crazy if each time I did that I wrote out "priest/pastor/deacon/minister/bishop, etc." I never liked the word "clergy" (it sounds too "religiousy" to me), so just for the sake of keeping things short and sweet, I chose one—pastor. It just sounds kind of folksy to me, which I like, but know that when I say that, it's just shorthand for "priest/pastor/deacon/minister/bishop, etc."

(8) I don't pretend to have all the answers. I can share what I've learned, and how it's affected me, my life, and the people around me, but I'll tell you right up front, sometimes the answer is simply, "I don't know." Luckily, if you feel you need more answers, there are at least 257,000 other books on this very topic.

This is the Last One. It's a Biggie

BILL FORTNEY

(9) So, exactly who is Jesus? My guess is this isn't the first time you've heard of Jesus, and so you've probably heard at some point that Jesus is God's Son (it's been fairly well-publicized). I'm not saying you believe it—I'm just saying you've probably heard it. In short, Jesus is the name He was given by His parents, but He is also known by a number of different names: the most common are Christ, or The Lord, or even Christ the Lord, but you'll also hear some folks refer to Him as The Messiah, or The Savior, or Steve (okay, they don't really call Him Steve. I just wanted to see if you're still paying attention). He lived here a couple thousand years ago, and He had a bigger impact on the course of world events than anyone in history. When He came here, He radically challenged the beliefs of the religious leaders at the time, which instantly made him a "marked man." Jesus spent most of His time here on earth literally trying to teach us how to get along with one another, how to live in peace together, how to take care of each other, and how to relate to God in a new way. The religious leaders at the time spent most of their time trying to arrest Him and/or kill Him, which they eventually did. Of course, you can't keep a good man down, and three days later, Jesus came back to life (in a historically documented event) to prove to everybody, once and for all, that He was sent from God. Now, there's more to Jesus than just this (as you'll learn throughout this book), but at this point, I thought you'd want to know that He was sent here from God and He lived an extraordinary life devoted to teaching us how to care for each other, and He died as part of a plan to make it so we could live happy, fulfilling lives here on earth and after (more on that later). Basically, He's "The Man!" (okay, that's an understatement, but you know what I mean). So, those are the "Nine Things" and now I think you're ready to start the book. Let's get to it, because you and I both have a lot at stake here.

Chapter One

Christian Stereotypes & Myths

We're Not All Crazy (Just the Crazy Ones)

Ever watch a football game on TV in December, where the game is being held at an outdoor stadium, where it's freezing cold (like 6° below zero—probably a Green Bay game), and the camera pans to some guy in the crowd with his shirt off, his face painted, and he's cheering at the top of his lungs? Yeah, that guy. Have you ever noticed that "that guy" is at every single sub-zero NFL game (but, of course, it's not the exact same guy, but another shirtless, freezing, frenzied football fan). These guys aren't your typical football fans (keeping in mind, that fan is short for fanatic). Sure there are 70,000+ regular fans with their shirts still on, and faces unpainted, but there's always a few of "that guy" in the stadium. But if they weren't football fans, and instead they were…say… *Star Trek* fans, you'd see them at the annual *Star Trek* convention dressed in full costume and makeup (my buddy Terry, a big *Star Trek* fan himself, always says, "Once you put on a costume, you've crossed the line"). Now, take that super-psyched, totally in-your-face type of personality, and turn them onto God. You'd get one of those wide-eyed, crazy-haired religious fanatics that run up to people, grab them by the shoulders and yell, "Have you been saved, brother?" Now, let's circle back. How many fans at the freezing-cold NFL game stand there with their shirts off? Right, not many. How many *Star Trek* fans go to the convention in full costume (okay, I'm not sure this answer will help my case)? Well, it's the same with people really into God—some people go totally over the top. Are all Christians like that? Absolutely not. Are most? Nope. Have you met a few in your life like that? I sure have. But they're the exception—not the rule. There are a lot of assumptions and stereotypes and myths you've probably heard that are either way outdated or just plain wrong. Luckily, hearing how things really are will help you breath a big sigh of relief.

1

You'll Have to Work Jesus Into Every Sentence

SCOTT KELBY

I know you've probably run into people who end each sentence with "Praise the Lord," or "Thank you, Jesus," or "Hallelujah," or one of a dozen other Christian taglines. Luckily (and thankfully), you will not be required to do this. In fact, if you do, you'll probably wind up annoying everyone around you (even some Christians). I always felt people say this stuff to let other people know they are "saved," and "tight with God," and all that stuff. I can't find any real purpose for why they do this, other than to look "Jesusy" to others (even Jesus didn't talk like that). This kind of stuff always makes me cringe, so know now, right up front, that not only is it not a requirement for becoming a Christian, it's annoying as $%&$.

You'll Need to Clean Up Your Language

BILL FORTNEY

You've probably met some Christians who use "colorful language." Take my assistant Kathy, for example. I never hear her use any foul language (she's the nicest person and a Christian, too). But, I went with her and her husband to a Washington Redskins game once, and I heard her say things that would make Andrew Dice Clay blush. Actually, she screamed them—at the players, at the coach, and at some of the refs—from 35 rows up. But it's not just her, it's all Redskins fans (just kidding—sorry, as a Buc's fan, I couldn't resist). Anyway, here's the thing: if you become a Christian, you won't have to sign an agreement promising to remove certain words from your vocabulary. Not using "cuss" words doesn't make you a Christian anymore than using them makes you a longshoreman. However, there are probably some words you might want to stop using altogether. For me, it was "GD." I used to sometimes say that phrase back when my wife and I were first dating, until one day she looked at me and said, "Do you really know what you're saying there?" I never used it again (that was 22+ years ago). Although my wife brought it to my attention, I stopped using that phrase because of my relationship with God. He has done so much for me, why would I ever use that phrase? Now, I don't usually cuss in everyday conversation, but if I was to slam my knee into a sharp corner of a table, for 30 seconds or so, I might sound like a Redskins fan (when they're behind seven points with less than two minutes left in the fourth quarter). So, in short, if you cut back or totally curtail cussing, it will be because something inside told you to—not because it's a rule.

You'll Start "Acting" Like a Christian

BILL FORTNEY

In your everyday life, there are people all around you that have a relationship with God, but you'd probably never know it. There are exceptions, of course—people who work Jesus into every conversation, carry a Bible everywhere they go, etc., but those aren't your average Christians. I think having a relationship with God will certainly make you a much happier person inside (and probably outside, as well), but it's a very personal thing, and if tonight you started developing a relationship with God, you won't wake up tomorrow yelling "Praise the Lord," or have the urge to dress up in a suit and go around with a wild look in your eyes like a Christian zombie. You are who you are. For example, one day you're a husband. The next day your wife has a baby and, at that moment, you're a dad. Your life has changed in a very profound way—you're not the person you were, but when you get back to work a few days later, you're just you. You don't look any different on the outside, but inside you're not just you—you're a dad. A father. A mentor. Half of a critically important team. And while your inside has changed immeasurably, your outside is still the same (except you're sleepy all the time. If you have a baby, not if you're a Christian. I just wanted to clarify that).

Your Friends Will Start Avoiding You

BILL FORTNEY

I've heard some people say they're concerned with how people will treat them if they become a Christian—that their friends and co-workers might feel uncomfortable around them and treat them differently. For example, if a golfing buddy goes to tell a bawdy joke, one of the group will say, "Not in front of Bob; he's a Christian." This will only happen if you go beyond just being a Christian, and decide to become "the Christianity police," correcting everything you see in others that you personally deem to be non-Christian-like. This is a really bad plan. Nobody wants you policing them, and you don't want people treating you differently, feeling uncomfortable around you, or avoiding you. The way to keep that from happening is to not be incredibly annoying about your new found love of Christ. There's no reason to hide it—I think it's the single greatest thing that can happen to a person—but there's also no reason to parade it around like you're the first person in history to uncover this amazing new discovery. Just chill out, and everybody will still enjoy being around you.

You'll Have to Go to Church Five Times a Week!

SCOTT KELBY

Although some folks get really into it, and want to go to church as much as possible (I know a couple that go every single day), I'd pretty much figure if you're going to hook up with a church, you should probably count on being there one day a week. If that sounds like a lot, just remember you're not there all day—probably just an hour or so. There are 168 hours in a week, and that means you're in church learning about God less than 1% of your time, leaving you more than 99% free to do all your un-God-like things (kidding). Many churches offer more than one service during the week, but I'm a Sunday morning guy myself (not the early service, though. It's the weekend, right?). That being said, you owe it to yourself to go every Sunday you possibly can because we tend to learn and grow through developing habits and doing things consistently (athletes are a great example—they grow and develop though repetition, consistency, and dedication—they can't be casual about working out and hope to be great athletes). So, get in the habit of going—in spending that 1% of your week learning about God. And don't worry if you can't make it one Sunday. They're not going to call you at home, or be your wake-up call. If they do call you, you picked the wrong church.

If You Do Go to Church, You'll Have to Dress Up

BRAD MOORE

If you choose a church where everybody dresses up on Sunday morning, then you'll probably want to dress up, too. But, here's the thing: you don't have to choose that church. Some people really enjoy the dressing-up aspect of going to church (after all, sometimes it's the only time we actually get dressed up, except for work), and some folks feel that wearing their "Sunday best" shows respect for God's house. I, on the other hand, feel like God will like me no matter what I'm wearing, and whether I wear a really fancy outfit, or I come in shorts and sneakers, it's not going to change how He feels about me, so I chose a church where they dress very casually. That casual dress code really appeals to me, so I'm more likely to be there every Sunday. Church isn't supposed to be a fashion show, and by choosing a church where they dress casually, you sidestep all the things like, "I can't go this week, because my suit isn't pressed," or "I've worn that dress too many times this month," or any other fashion-related issues. Also, I can go to my church after most anything. If my son has a soccer game first thing in the morning, I can go to the second service at my church right after, without going home to change clothes first. So, choose a church whose dress code fits your style, and you'll feel more comfortable when you're there.

You'll Have to Dress Like a Christian

BILL FORTNEY

There is no official dress code for Christians. You don't have to wear a cross around your neck, you don't have to wear sensible shoes, you don't have to slap a Jesus fish bumper sticker on your car, or wear a WWJD (What Would Jesus Do) bracelet around your wrist. You don't have to change your "look" at all. It's not about what's on the outside—it's your inside that will do all the changing.

You'll Have to Switch to Christian Music

BRAD MOORE

Your musical tastes are unlikely to change if you become a Christian. If you like Green Day, you're still going to like Green Day (well, I like Green Day anyway). The one thing you might do is finally pause on that Christian rock radio station that you always cruise right by and actually give it a listen, now that the words have some real meaning to you. You'll soon find, as many of us have, that there are some really incredible Christian bands (like the band NEEDTOBREATHE, in the image above), as well as, some really, really awful Christian bands, but either way, there's no requirement to listen to Christian music. One thing I have noticed about Christian music is that because the range of topics is pretty limited, the lyrics to a lot of Christian songs, are…well…you'll see what I mean. Also, today's Christian music is much different than you might imagine as it comes in a wide variety of styles from metal to hip/hop, from pop to country, from alternative to reggae, from funk to blues, and well…pretty much every style you can think of. At times in my life, I've listened to both regular and Christian music at the same time, and the cool thing about all this is you get to enjoy a new genre of music—you don't have to trade out or swap one of your favorite bands for a Christian band. In fact, you don't ever have to listen to a Christian band. Ever. Listening to them doesn't make you a Christian, and not listening to them doesn't penalize you. Did I mention the lyrics?

The Church is Full of Hypocrites

SCOTT KELBY

Sadly, there are some churches that are more like a club, where people who act like they're all perfect, and don't commit any sins, get dressed up and get together each week to pat each other on the back about being a "chosen one." If that's your experience with a church, then yes—that church is packed full of hypocrites. But, that's certainly not all churches, and that's not how many of us see church to begin with. I see church as "God college." It's a place where people who don't know everything about God go to learn. For example, if you were to enroll in medical school as a freshman, you'd find that it wouldn't be full of genius doctors, it's full of students—people who are just learning about medicine, who make mistakes, who mess up, and who still have a lot to learn about medicine. That's pretty much like church. It's not full of perfect people. It's full of people who are still learning about God. They make mistakes, they mess up, they have a lot to learn about God, and this is the place where they go to learn more. If you choose to go to church, you'll find that the people there are just like you. They're your friends, and co-workers, and they're just there to learn about God, even if they mess up during the week, and make the same mistakes again and again. They're not hypocrites—they're just getting a weekly reminder to try and do better the next week. To learn why they messed up last week, and the reason why they should help other people this week. That's not a bad thing.

You'll Turn Into a Bible-Quoting Fanatic

BILL FORTNEY

There's no requirement to memorize or quote Bible passages, and you don't have to work them into your conversations. In fact, I'm hoping you won't ever be tempted to do that. It's like people who work French into everyday conversation—they just want the person they're talking with to think, "Hey, they know French." Same thing with quoting Bible verses. Most Christians don't quote Bible verses in daily conversation and you won't be expected to either. Now, your pastor (minister, priest, etc.) might work in these phrases because, well…they're professionals, but for you and me—we're totally off the hook.

Christians Don't Have as Much Fun

SCOTT KELBY

Christians have as much fun as anybody else, so don't think that if you become a Christian, "the party's over." You can still dance, enjoy an ice cold beer or a glass of wine, go to your local bar, drive a nice car, see R-rated movies, etc., unless (and this is a big unless), you choose a particular denomination that doesn't allow those things (and there are a few). If you want a reason not to have any fun, choose one of those few denominations where fun is a no-no. Now, even though Christians have as much fun as anybody else, that doesn't mean that at some point you might want to make some changes in your life to strengthen your relationship with God. Just know that God will let you know what, when, if, and how to change—not somebody at your church that has appointed themselves to be the "pleasure police." Jesus, Himself, had some harsh things to say to religious leaders who tried to impose their regulations on people. In fact, I believe they are the only people he ever condemned.

All the Church Cares About is Money

BILL FORTNEY

There is no initiation fee, registration fee, or club dues required to become a Christian—not a single dollar. That being said, if you do decide to join a church, I would definitely pitch a few bucks in to help out. It's not because churches are greedy (okay, there are a few notable exceptions), but it's simply because running a church these days is more expensive than you can imagine. Churches rely totally on the donations of the people who attend regularly, and if people don't give, bills stack up, the electricity goes off, the lawn doesn't get mowed, there's no toilet paper (gasp!), salaries of the people who work full time at the church don't get paid, and so on. Now, devoted members of a church often do donate 10% of their gross earnings to the church—not only because they feel they should, but because they're investing in the future of their community, and of this world. Churches do amazing things. They are usually the first on the scene to help when there's a crisis, and especially when nobody else will (not the government, not politicians). This is worth supporting. So, while I've never been to a church where giving 10% is a requirement for attendance, there are probably a few churches out there that do require it, so when you're "church shopping," find out about that policy right up front. I will tell you this, though: everyone I know that does give 10% off the top will tell you the same story—since they started doing it, their financial fortunes have greatly changed for the better. Maybe it's a total coincidence. Maybe not. But either way, it's absolutely not a requirement for becoming a believer, so don't let anyone tell you it is.

You Won't Be Able to Do Things on the Sabbath

SCOTT KELBY

Most Christians do the same things on Sunday that everybody else does. Some work on Sunday. Some go to the beach, the mall, or to the county fair. They drink beer watching the football game or NASCAR. For most Christians, Sunday is the day they go to church, and spend time with their family, but outside of that, it's just another weekend day. The whole idea of the Sabbath was that it was a gift from God to give us a break from all the craziness of the work week. It was supposed to be a time to break from our normal routine, to be with our family, to relax and get rested up, and to do stuff we don't have time to do the rest of the week. To spend some unhurried time with God, enjoy meals with your family and friends, and basically have a one-day vacation each week. It was never intended to be a day just spent in church and doing nothing but church-related activities. Also, you don't ever have to use the word "Sabbath" or worry about the "sanctity of the Sabbath" or any of that stuff unless you choose a denomination that is sticky about that.

You'll Have to Recruit Others

BILL FORTNEY

This is not a multi-level marketing scheme, where the success of the program relies upon recruiting others. This is between you and God, so you don't have to worry about getting "distributors" (well, pastors do maybe, but not you). That being said, you've probably run into friends, co-workers, etc., that are so over the top about their relationship with God that it seems like they've got a monthly quota to fill. It may be hard, but try and think of these people as if they just saw an incredible movie, and now they want to tell every-body about it. I'm like that—if I find a great new restaurant, I email my friends saying, "You've got to try this new Thai place." So, I kind of understand (on some level). But now take it up a notch. They didn't just see a great movie—these people have had their entire lives transformed. They had something standing between them and real happiness, and all of sudden that wall is gone, and they're finally happy inside. They're experiencing kind of a euphoric joy, and they can't wait to tell everybody about this great new thing in their lives. This is why Christians always seem to want other people to become Christians—they want to share this awesome thing they've discovered, and they genuinely want you to be as psyched as they are. The problem is, sometimes they get so psyched that they're kind of like a big, happy sheepdog that comes bounding at you and jumps into your lap, licking your face, and you just want to take a bone and toss it as far away from you as you can, so they'll leave you alone even for a moment. But then they bring the slobbery bone right back into your lap and start licking your face again. I try to cut these people some slack (but I keep a bag of doggie bones within arm's reach at all times).

You'll Have to Stop Having Premarital Sex

SCOTT KELBY

Only if you're not married (wink wink). Now, you already know the answer to this one, right? It's pretty obvious. I mean, come on…you know, or you wouldn't be asking me. It's like asking, "Do I have to quit stealing to become a Christian?" You so know the answer. That being said, here's the thing: having premarital sex won't keep you from becoming a Christian and having premarital sex *after* becoming a Christian won't get you kicked out of the special Christian club (which doesn't exist, by the way). However, once you become a Christian, you'll want to be a better person, and you'll want to grow your closeness and relationship to God, so I imagine at some point, you'll realize that living this way isn't helping you on that path, and it's not helping the person you love either. You'll realize that it's just not right for you any longer. Just living with someone was not God's plan (that's one reason He created marriage), and you may find yourself looking differently at a lot of things that before didn't seem like a big deal to you. Like premarital sex.

You'll Start Telling People You're "Born Again"

SCOTT KELBY

"Born again" is basically kind of an outdated Christian way of saying your old life is behind you in such a big way (now that you believe in Jesus) that it's almost like being born all over again (babies start with a clean state, right? They don't have any moral baggage or things they don't want anyone to know about in their past, and so on). Also, this phrase wasn't used by people who had grown up knowing Jesus—it was for people who found Jesus later in life (you might have heard these people described as "born-again Christians," but again, you don't really hear that phrase too often today). The "saved" thing isn't really a term you'll use either—it's more likely one you've heard someone else use, as in "Have you been saved?" (as in, have you been saved from hell? Have you been saved from a life without meaning, have you found Jesus, etc.). Now, if that sent a little chill down your spine, it's probably because in movies when they want to portray a religious fanatic, that person is always running around asking everybody "Have you been saved, brother?" Luckily, that's mostly just in the movies. Sadly, it's not always just in the movies. Anyway, that's what those mean, but luckily, you're not required to ever use those phrases about yourself or anyone else.

Chapter Two
What's in It for Me?
Benefits of Becoming a Believer

 friend of mine has been a bachelor most of his life. He met this really great girl, and they had been dating for a few years, but he just wouldn't consider marrying her. Nobody could understand why he wouldn't marry her—she was wonderful, everybody loved her, he loved her—and when I asked him about it, he said he just wasn't ready to give up his bachelor life. Now, he isn't some young guy cruising the bars every night—this guy is in his late 40s, and I'll bet he hasn't been in a nightclub in 10 years—and hasn't dated any other woman for years now. When my wife heard this, she said, "Seriously, what is he giving up—sitting at home alone at night in his underwear watching sports?" She kinda had a point there (of course, if he had married that girl he dated, she would have gladly let him sit around in his underwear watching sports anyway, but at least he wouldn't be alone). Anyway, this chapter is kind of about something like that. My friend would have gained a lot by marrying that girl (a partner, a companion, someone who is always on his side and has his best interests at heart, someone to take care of him, watch over him, worry about him, and love him. Someone to travel with, laugh with, cry with, and do life with). He had everything to gain, and nothing to lose but the loneliness. When you turn the page, we'll look at all the things you have to gain by becoming a Christian, yet you only have to give up…well…nothing. It doesn't cost money, you don't have to do a bunch of good deeds, and you don't have to sign a contract. The whole thing is a very private process, just between you and God. You have an awful lot to gain, and nothing to lose.

You Get to Start Over with a Clean Slate

SCOTT KELBY

I think one of the most compelling reasons to become a Christian is that you get to start over with a clean slate, because part of the process in becoming a Christian is asking God to forgive you for the bad things you've done in your past (called "sins" in Christian talk). And the great thing is—He will. His forgiveness is the basis that being a Christian is built upon (as you'll see in just a few minutes), so if you did bad stuff in your past (even really bad stuff), now you can start over fresh because God will forgive you. Totally. Completely. That's what makes His forgiveness so amazing. What you did before doesn't need to define who you are going forward. You can't change what you've done in the past, but you can absolutely change the future, and starting off forgiven, with a completely clean slate, is your best chance for changing your life from here on out.

You Are Able to Forgive

BILL FORTNEY

When you've been forgiven by God, it makes you much more open to forgiving other people for things they've done to you. The weird thing about forgiveness is that it's as much for you as the person you're forgiving (in fact, probably more). The person that caused you pain may not even realize it, and even if they're the guilty party, they've already gone on with their life. They're not sitting around their apartment, hands in the air, saying, "I can't believe I broke up with that wonderful woman and hurt her, three girlfriends ago." They've moved on and you may not even cross their mind at all. Ever. They may intentionally not want to think about you, or about how they treated you, so you're basically "out of sight, out of mind." But yet, you still feel that pain that they caused. How do you get rid of that pain? Forgive them. Totally. Completely. So, while a big part of all this is the forgiveness you get, in the long run it'll be your ability to now forgive others that will impact your life the most on a daily basis. Right now, at this stage in your life, it might seem impossible for you to really forgive someone who did something to you that still causes you pain. If you're thinking, "I just can't do that. You don't know what they did to me—how much hurt they caused," then you need this more than you know. Just remember, you won't be forgiving them for their sake, you're doing it for you. You don't even have to tell them you've forgiven them (especially since they probably haven't even given it another thought), so it really is for you, and like I said, once you've been forgiven by God, forgiving others becomes dramatically easier.

It Fills a Hole Inside You Other Things Can't Fill

BILL FORTNEY

A lot of people feel something is missing in their life. They usually don't know exactly what it is, but they know something isn't quite right and so they try to fill it with something. Some people try drinking, drugs, or sex. Some people think if they just had that bigger car, or that blingy piece of jewelry, or a trophy wife, then they'd be happy. So, they wind up accumulating a lot of "stuff," but find that they're still not happy. That hole is still there, which makes them feel even worse. Here's the thing: I believe we were meant to have a relationship with our Maker. We're weren't born to be a Godless race, wandering aimlessly through life. Our lives were meant to having meaning, and that hole you keep trying to fill was put there by God, and it can only be filled by having a relationship with Him. That's what's missing inside you. That's why nothing else you try to get rid of that "empty" feeling inside ever seems to work. When you become a Christian, it fills that hole inside where Jesus was missing. You're not empty inside any longer, and your life will finally have real meaning. Just don't expect a sudden bolt of lightning, or that you'll wake up one morning and you'll have that wide-eyed look that scares the living crap out of everyone around you. This is a gradual process, but once you find "it," you'll know. Ask anyone who knows. Building a relationship with God is what fills that hole.

It Gives Meaning and Purpose to Your Life

SCOTT KELBY

Ever ask yourself, "What's the meaning of my life?" You're not alone. Is it to get a job, work hard, take a two-week vacation each year, and then after a while you die? Does that sound like a life with meaning? With purpose? Is there more to life than that, or is that pretty much it? If that sounds like a pretty shallow, meaningless existence, I totally agree. In between all that work, can't we have fulfilling lives that extend beyond buying the latest fashions or a bigger TV? Absolutely. I believe God has a custom-made plan for each of us, that thing that He put us here for, the thing that gives us true joy, and a true sense that what you do matters, and makes a difference. Unfortunately, a lot of us don't ever stop to learn what God's plan for us is, and we just go along with our own plan instead, which for most is that whole working-until-you-die thing. So, how do you find out what God's plan is for you? You've already started that journey. If you do nothing more than read this book, you've at least aimed your ear in God's direction. Whether you become a Christian, and get close enough to hear God, is really up to you (I'm speaking metaphorically here). When you do find out God's plan for you, don't be surprised if His plan isn't for you to sell all your belongings and become a missionary in Africa. He may need you to be at "the right place at the right time" to make a big difference in someone's life who lives right next door, or down the street, or even a co-worker. Becoming a Christian is the first step in finding out the meaning of your life, and why you're here in the first place. But, you've got to take the first step.

You're No Longer Going It Alone

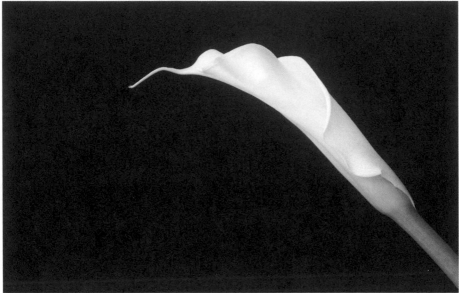

SCOTT KELBY

When you're watching the news and you see someone who's been kidnapped, or been held in captivity under some horrible conditions, and the reporter asks them how they survived, you'll almost always hear the same story—that it was their faith in God that got them through it. They knew they weren't alone. At some point in your life, you've probably felt alone (but, hopefully not "held hostage"), and that's probably because you were. Going it alone is tough, and feeling like you're alone is even worse, but it doesn't have to be that way. You don't have to do this all alone. I know it sounds kind of corny reading it here in a book, but once Jesus is in your life, you won't feel alone inside anymore. You'll know that He wants the best for you and that He's on your team. He wants you to succeed at this. This isn't the Green Beret test where they're trying to weed you out (and only the strongest survive). This is more like a father trying to help his daughter on a math test. You want her to succeed, right? You want her to ace the test, and when she does, it's a win for both of you. God's the same way. He's not waiting up there for you to screw up, so He can slap you with a plague. He wants you to win at life. He's pulling for you. He's there to open doors for you, to make opportunities appear, to help you along the way, to coach you and show you which path to take. He's not setting you up for failure—He's there to show you the road to real success in your life. God's not just "the big guy upstairs" watching you drown from shore and yelling "Swim!" He jumps in and saves you.

You'll Be in Good Company

BILL FORTNEY

If you eventually do decide to become a Christian, you'll be in some pretty good company (in fact, a recent *ABC News* poll showed that 83% of Americans identify themselves as Christians, which kind of freaked me out because that vastly lowers the number of people this book can help, until I realized that the remaining 17% represent nearly 53 million people. But, of course, within that 17% are people who are Jewish, Muslim, and other religions, so it's actually less). Now, there was probably a point in history where naming past U.S. presidents would be a good example here, but looking back at what's happened in the past 20 or so years, I know you would just start giggling. So, instead, let's look at some of the brave firefighters who raced into the burning World Trade Center towers on September 11, 2001. While everybody else was running out, they were running in, and that takes a level of courage and commitment most of us will never know. It takes faith that what you're doing is right. Taking a job with little pay, and high-personal risk is something you're called from inside to do (by the way—who do you think is doing that calling?). You'll find committed Christians in all walks of life—they're in every branch of our Armed Forces, they're teachers, police officers, movie stars, rock musicians, celebrity chefs, airline pilots, TV show hosts, radio disc jockeys, factory workers, surgeons, circus performers, soccer moms, scientists, star athletes, and everybody in between. Anyway, no matter what profession, what walk of life, what economic situation, you'll be in good company because some of the best, coolest, most fascinating, and most fun people on the planet are Christians.

Your Final Destination Will Be Heaven

BILL FORTNEY

So, where are you going when you die? I know, first a quick stop at the funeral home, but then where? Is that it? Is that the end? Is there more? If you're not sure, then you can definitely count this on the plus side for becoming a Christian, because this is one of the main reasons to become a Christian—to finally know, in your heart of hearts, exactly where you're going when you die. Because when you believe in Jesus, you're going to heaven. Look at any poll on dying, and you'll see that a vast majority of people feel certain that there's something else after we leave this earth. The problem is— many have no idea what. They're taking a roll of the dice—hoping it's good and if it is, hoping they're invited. Hope isn't a great strategy to bet your eternity upon. Look back on your life, on things you've hoped would happen (I hope I win the lottery, I hope the most popular girl/guy in high school will somehow fall madly in love with me, I hope I get that promotion, etc.). How many times did it work out exactly as you had hoped? I'm a great believer in positive thinking, and I think hope is a great thing (for example, I hope you really find this book helpful), but if you knew a way to turn hope into results, wouldn't you do it? Exactly. When you become a Christian, you turn that hope into a reality. You'll know where you're going—you've done exactly what it takes to get into heaven (but you still won't know when, so I wouldn't sit on this one for too long).

We Have Some Really Awesome Holidays

SCOTT KELBY

Even if you're not a Christian, you've probably celebrated Christmas. It's an awesome holiday, celebrated all over the world, even by people who aren't Christians, because it's just the coolest holiday ever. You've probably put up a Christmas tree, exchanged gifts, and sang Christmas carols, but if you're reading this and thinking "Yeah, but it's gotten so commercialized and so hyped," then it's probably because that's all it is to you—buying and getting stuff. When you become a Christian, you'll still have a tree, exchange gifts, and all that, but now it will be a real celebration, and all that commercialization stuff fades into the background, and the real reason for the season (the birth of Jesus) comes to the front. It will truly transform your Christmases going forward. Also, there's Easter. You'll still want your Cadbury chocolate eggs, but now this holiday will have real meaning for you. Even Thanksgiving will change for you, because now you'll have a whole lot more to be thankful for. Holidays will take on new meaning, and they'll go from a few days off work to a celebration of the things that God has done for you in your life. (By the way, I didn't mention St. Patrick's Day, which is a Christian feast to honor the Patron Saint of Ireland, St. Patrick. But, we all know that you don't need to be Christian, or Irish, or anything other than someone with a pulse to celebrate this holiday, which is celebrated by virtually anyone within seven nautical miles of a bar. I can't honestly tell you St. Patrick's Day will mean anything more to you after becoming a Christian, but when you wake up with a hangover the next day, now at least you'll have someone to pray to that it goes away fast. Just kidding!)

You Become Part of a Solution

SCOTT KELBY

When you hear people talking about "the church," they're not talking about the building. "The church" is the people who go there. While you might only hear from the pastor on Sunday, if there's a crisis in your community, your state, or somewhere else in your country or even the world, it's the people in your church that will be the ones who come to the rescue first. Before the government, before the insurance companies—before anybody. The actual "feet on the ground" during a crisis and the people on the scene first to help will be the churchgoers themselves. When the Gulf Coast was devastated by Hurricane Katrina, thousands of churches all across the U.S., and even from other countries, sent immediate help. They set up relief centers providing food, clothing, and comfort to people they had never met, and would never see again. That's what churches do. Here it is years later, and a number of churches are actually still there helping to rebuild homes and lives to this very day. When you become a Christian, and you join a church, you become part of the only real hope for this world. You become part of the solution. Surprisingly, you'll learn that giving that help will actually make you feel better than the people you're helping and it lifts you up in a way you can't imagine.

You Get to Do Life with Some Cool People

BRAD MOORE

You probably have a preconceived notion of how Christians act, because, like I've mentioned, you've no doubt met some Christians who are "mega Christians" and end every sentence with "Praise the Lord." But, you'll find out that most Christians aren't mega Christians—they're just regular people like you and me, and you'll wind up creating some of the best, most meaningful, and real relationships you've ever had. Part of it is that you'll have something in common with a massive group of people around the world, who all kind of look out for each other, and usually when you find people who share some kind of common bond, it draws you together. Some of the coolest people I've ever met are Christians, and you'll meet some really cool people, too. This is something that surprises a lot of new Christians—they find out that regular Christians are...well...regular. You're going to click with at least some of these people, and form friendships that will last a lifetime.

You'll Have a Place to Go in Times of Crisis

BILL FORTNEY

When do people go to church most? When they feel they need it. Generally, when people experience a major crisis or transition in their life, they head for church. Like when they have a serious health crisis, or if they get divorced, lose their job, or when they have a financial crisis. After 9/11, churches were literally packed, because people were looking for a place where there was hope. People look at church as a place where they can find answers to things in life that just don't make sense—they want stability and reassurance, and for literally thousands of years the church has been there. It's where people turn when they're feeling worried or alone. Think of it this way: when there's a political or economic crisis in the world, investors start buying gold (pushing the price of gold up, which by the way, is currently near its all-time high), because investors know that if all hell breaks loose, and currencies get devalued, gold will still hold its worth. It's considered a safe haven in times of financial trouble. For literally thousands of years, the church has been that same thing—a safe haven, a place where people go to find stability, and look for answers to things in life that just don't make sense. It's where you turn when all hell breaks loose in your life and your world is unravelling. Thankfully, you don't have to wait until you're in a personal or financial crisis to surround yourself with that same hope, reassurance, and stability. You can have that in your life every single day.

Why I Haven't Told You You're Going to Hell

SCOTT KELBY

That's implied. You're going to hell. (Kidding. I hope.) For one thing, it's because I don't think you are. I don't think you are because you're holding this book. The fact that you're reading this means you're on a path toward building a real relationship with God and His Son, Jesus. It may be a very small path at this point, but at least you're here. You're asking questions. You're curious. That's a good thing. Besides, I don't want to scare you into believing in Jesus. Instead, I want to show you all the benefits of becoming a Christian (someone who believes in Jesus)—how it's going to transform your life, and give you real direction, a sense of purpose, and guidance to help you along the way. I might not know you personally, but I love people (I'm kind of a people person), and I would be thrilled for you if you wound up having a rich, happy, and fulfilling life because you became a Christian, and I don't think telling you you're going to burn in hell forever is the way to do that. That is, unless you think telling you that would help (kidding). By the way, you've probably run across people who sometimes make jokes about how they're "going to hell." Maybe it's because on some level, in their private moments, they know they are.

You'll "Get" the Whole "Inner Peace" Thing

BILL FORTNEY

People throw around the "you'll know inner peace" thing, but what does it really mean? Well, think about it this way: I've been married for 22 years to an absolutely awesome woman. No matter what, she's always on my side. She's always looking out for me and genuinely has my best interests at heart. Even if I make mistakes, she helps me past them and doesn't condemn me. She'll stick up for me when nobody else will. She's always there for me. Always. When you have a real sense of security, of belonging, it gives you tremendous satisfaction and confidence to face any challenge, because you know you're not facing it alone. It's also why when marriages (or long-term relationships) break up, people freak out. That security is gone and now they're empty and alone. Think back on your own life to a painful break up you had with someone you loved and how empty, lost, and hopeless you felt when the relationship ended. You'd do anything to get that person back, right? Anything to get that feeling of belonging, of security, of (say it with me) inner peace back (ahhh, now it makes sense). Now, let's take that and apply it to your relationship with God. If you have either broken away from God, or never formed a relationship with Him, maybe that's why you feel the way you do. Why you might feel empty and alone. And it's why you need to start, or re-establish your relationship with God, so you'll have that feeling inside that someone is always there looking out for you, genuinely has your best interests at heart, and if you make mistakes, helps you get past them and doesn't condemn you. Inner peace can be a real thing for you and is a huge benefit of becoming a Christian.

Chapter Three

So Who is This Jesus Guy?
And What's All the Fuss About?

 ike I mentioned earlier, I know you've probably already heard that Jesus claimed to be the Son of God (you knew that before you ever got your hands on this book), and you might have even heard that He was sent here a long time ago to fix the huge mess we had ourselves in (well, that was one reason, but as you'll read in this chapter, there are more reasons). But, of course, there's a lot more to Him than just that, so I wanted to give you some insight into the life He led here on earth and some of the things He did while He was here. He was a remarkable person (which I know is a huge understatement when you're talking about God's Son, right?), but I think what you'll find in these next pages was that He was very different and did things in a very different way (teaching-wise, example-wise, and so on) that really made Him stand out in a way that won Him lots of loyal followers, but also drew lots of people who literally wanted to kill Him (and eventually they did). Speaking of Jesus dying, for people who aren't Christians, it sometimes seems a little weird that the thing we use to symbolize Jesus is the very cross He died on (I mean, you wouldn't wear an electric chair on a necklace around your neck, right?), but you see Christians wearing the cross on necklaces all the time. That's because to us it doesn't symbolize death, it symbolizes the sacrifice that God made for us by sending His Son to die on that cross. That act reminded the world how much God truly loves us—so much that He would sacrifice His own Son for us. For our happiness. For our future. I can tell you as a father of two myself, it's a sacrifice I cannot imagine. Okay, enough sad stuff—let's go learn about the most important guy ever!

35

Remember That Movie, *10,000 BC*?

SCOTT KELBY

Take a look at your calendar. What's today's date? As I write this book, it's 2011. But this planet and its documented history is more than 2,011 years old, right? So what was year one? It was the year Jesus was born. That's right, the calendar the entire world uses each day, from India to China, from Egypt to France, from Ottawa to Kenya is numbered starting when Jesus was born. His birth is such a part of our planet's recorded history, that it's the worldwide standard for the measurement for time (his birth literally split the history of time in two). In that movie *10,000 BC*, the BC doesn't stand for "British Columbia." That BC part stands for "Before Christ." AD is an abbreviation for the term "Anno Domini," which is Latin for "in the year of our Lord". Isn't that wild? We measure our planet's history around one man's life. What a history changer, huh!

Why He Came Here in the First Place

SCOTT KELBY

When God created us, He had a pretty good idea of how He wanted things to play out, so we could have a relationship with Him, and lead happy, fulfilling lives in the world He created for us. He wanted us to look out for each other, to live in peace, to care for one another, and so on. When I mentioned the "live in peace" part, you probably thought "Uh oh," because that's just one way we've gotten way off track from the life God had planned for us. Instead, we started to look for happiness through money, through sex, through buying stuff, and I imagine if you're reading this, you've already learned that those aren't the things that truly make people happy (if they were, you'd be reading one of those "Get rich quick, so you can buy stuff to attract people who might have sex with you" books). Those things don't bring long-term happiness or ful-fillment or lasting relationships. So, God sent Jesus here as an example for us to follow. He was sent to show us that life's not about accumulating stuff, but about the things that make life really great—it's about building relationships, looking out for each other, enjoying the natural beauty around us, real love, helping the poor, and caring for those less fortunate than us. These are the things that give your life real purpose and mean-ing. He was sent to let us know that there's a reason why we're on this earth in the first place (and it's not just to see how much stuff we can buy and how much money we can have in the bank). He was here to teach us to have compassion, to show us the way, and give us hope for the future. He wasn't just here to show us how to get to heaven. He was here to show us how to have a little bit of heaven here on earth.

He Was More Than a Prophet

SCOTT KELBY

You know the magazine *O*? It's Oprah Winfrey's magazine (and a pretty good maga-zine) and there are editors at *O* that take her vision for what she wants in her maga-zine, and they bring it to the readers. When you read *O* you can feel Oprah's influence, and you get her message, but it's a whole lot different than meeting her and having a conversation with her, right? Well, back in the day, there were prophets, who were peo-ple that felt they had been spoken to by God and now they were speaking on behalf of Him. God sent them as watchmen—to stand on the wall and warn people against making bad decisions and doing bad things. They were there to sound warnings about the future (more like, "If you continue to do immoral things, your lives will be ruined," rather than "Thursday you're going to Starbucks to order a mocha latte, but the barista will forget to steam the milk"). But they weren't God. They were just passing on God's vision (kind of like how Oprah's editors pass on her vision, but of course, I'm not trying to compare Oprah and God, because I think Oprah actually has more money). Any-way, when Jesus starting His teaching, some people were like, "Oh, he's just another prophet, predicting the future. Blah, blah, blah." But they soon realized He wasn't a prophet. He wasn't just another person passing on God's vision. He was God here on earth. It was God's word, God's plan, delivered in a way and with an authority that no one had done before or since. It's the difference between listening to U2 on the radio, and having Bono pull up a chair in front of you while he sings "It's a Beautiful Day" to you. When you hear it straight from the source, it's a whole different experience.

He Was an Awesome Teacher

BILL FORTNEY

Think back to when you were in school. I'll bet you can still name your favorite teacher. That one teacher that was different than all the rest. But what made that teacher impact you the most? Well, she (or he) probably explained things in a way that finally made sense to you. I imagine she had a real passion for teaching, and you could see it in everything she taught. You could see that she really cared about what you were learning, and you knew she wasn't teaching just to get a pay check—she was genuine. She was real. She loved teaching, and that came through in everything she taught. She had a real impact on your life, and teachers like her are very special people (and that's why you still remember her [or him] to this very day). Jesus was that same way. His teachings were totally different than the religious teachers at that time. His style of teaching made sense to people and his passion, his delivery, and his message was so different from anything they had heard before, and it really resonated with people. But what freaked everybody out was that He taught with such authority. He was genuine. He was the real deal. He was transforming lives. He was saying things the other teachers either couldn't or wouldn't say. He talked about things nobody else was talking about. He challenged the strict rules and man-made authority of the time (which didn't go over very big with local religious leaders, as you'll soon read) and He had such amazingly to-the-point examples and analogies that scholars around the world still study His teachings more than 2,000 year later. He wasn't just a teacher. He was *the* teacher.

He is Why There is Christmas

BILL FORTNEY

Christmas is the day we celebrate Jesus' birth. It's why there is a Christmas at all (I guess the fact that "Christ" is in the name probably tipped you off, eh?), and December 25th is the day chosen by most Christian denominations to celebrate His birth (though, it may not be the actual day He was born, which was more than 2,000 years ago, so you can forgive them for being off by a bit). I know what you're thinking, "Oh man, if He was born on Christmas day, that means he got rooked out of birthday presents every year." Don't worry, He didn't miss out on any presents, because while he was alive, there was no Christmas. It was just His birthday. In fact, Christmas wasn't celebrated until about 300 or so years after Jesus' death, but of course, today it's celebrated all over the world. Although different religions and denominations have their own special Christmas traditions (and some even celebrate it on different dates), they all celebrate it for the same reason—the birth of Jesus. How cool is that!

He Made a Lot of People Really Mad

BRAD MOORE

Although a lot of people loved Jesus, religious leaders pretty much hated Him. Mostly because His teachings were in direct contrast to all their strict religious rules. It was these rules that gave them control and power over the people, and of course they didn't want anybody messing with that, so they saw Jesus as a threat (especially after Jesus told people that their strict rules weren't what made you right with God). For example, the religious leaders were really strict about nobody working on the Sabbath (a holy day of rest and reflection each week), but if on the Sabbath Jesus came across someone who was sick, He healed them. Of course, this made those leaders furious. In fact, they tried to set Jesus up once by putting a sick guy in front of Him on the Sabbath. They knew that even though it was forbidden, He couldn't resist healing this poor guy. They were right. He couldn't resist and they used His healing on the Sabbath as public proof He was a bad guy—so bad that perhaps He should be put to death. So, while He did make a lot of people mad while He was here on earth, it was because His teachings were about love, compassion, and caring, and not about strict obedience to rules created by leaders. Jesus' goal wasn't to take control of the people—He was here to show us how to have a real relationship with God, and lead happy fulfilling lives because of it. By the way, I think one of the coolest things about Jesus was when He did heal the sick. He always called them away from the crowd, healing them in private, and then He told them, "Don't tell anyone I did this." He didn't want the power and the fame that comes with all that. He just wanted to help. That's my kind of guy!

He Hung Out with the "Wrong Type"

BRAD MOORE

Another thing Jesus did that drove the religious leaders at the time absolutely crazy was He spent time with what they thought were "the wrong element," including prostitutes, criminals, and so on. Those leaders felt like if Jesus was really the Son of God, He'd want to be hanging out with the religious leaders themselves and other dignitaries—basically surrounding Himself with holy and important people, just like they did. So why did Jesus hang out with these "bad" people? Because they needed Him the most. They needed His teachings. They needed to get their lives back on track. They needed His help. Jesus didn't want to waste His short time here on earth hanging around people who were already doing well and leading happy, moral lives. Those folks were already "on board" and didn't need His help. He wanted to be with people who were way off track—people He could rescue from a life of misery and pain. He chose them because these were people whose lives He could transform, and He treated these people with dignity, value, and respect because Jesus knew they mattered to God, and if they mattered to God, they mattered to Him.

You Can't Keep a Good Man Down!

SCOTT KELBY

Although Jesus did perform some miracles here on earth, He felt He needed to do something that would, once and for all, prove to everyone that He was indeed the Son of God—something no one else had ever done, or would ever do again. So, He basically told the leaders, point blank, that if they killed Him, three days later He would be alive again—something only God himself could pull off. Well, sure enough, they killed Jesus by nailing Him to a cross, and the Romans officially certified His death. They took His body and put it in a burial cave with a massive stone covering the entrance with a squad of soldiers standing guard outside 24/7, so nobody could sneak in and take the body and then try to claim Jesus had risen from the dead. But, sure enough, three days later, the tomb was empty. Literally, hundreds of eye witnesses saw Jesus alive and well. Juries even today find that one single eyewitness account is very hard to refute in court, so imagine trying to refute hundreds of eyewitnesses. Not that the leaders at the time didn't try—they rounded them up and tried to persuade them to recant what they saw by taking all their possessions, imprisoning them, burning some at the stake, and literally feeding some to the lions. But the people saw what they saw, and it was too late—too many people saw it with their own eyes and some felt so strongly about what they had seen that they gave their lives for it. So, it happened just as Jesus said it would. It was this resurrection that provided the irrefutable proof everyone was looking for, and it's precisely why we celebrate Easter to this day. It's not a celebration of the day Jesus died—it's the day we celebrate when Jesus proved once and for all He was the Son of God.

Chapter Four

At This Point, You Need to Find a Church

How to Find the Right One and What to Do Once You Get There

I know, I know, you're probably thinking, "Whoa Scott, I never said I was going to church." Hey, you do not have to go to church, ever, at all, not even once, to become a Christian, so don't sweat it. But consider this: If you wanted to learn how to play the guitar, you'd probably find a place that gives guitar lessons, right? So, where do you go for lessons about God? Church. There's a free lesson there every Sunday. If you're really interested in learning about God, this is really the next step. It's why people go to church in the first place (well, it's the main reason. The other is the promise of yummy snacks). Anyway, if you've read this book up to this point, at the very least I would say that your chances of going to a church one day soon have increased pretty dramatically, so if you do go, I want to make sure of two things: (1) That you pick the right church—one that fits you. Finding the right church, one where you feel comfortable, is critically important because if you're not comfortable, and if they're not teaching about God the way you need to learn (and if you don't "click" with them), you're probably not going back. And (2) when you do go, you'll know where to go, what to do, what to look out for, and generally how to act so you'll be comfortable. This is a bigger thing than you'd think, and the fear of doing something wrong, or not fitting in, is one of the major reasons why people don't go to church in the first place. So, I cover all that stuff in this chapter. Luckily, like in the stereotypes and myths chapter, a lot of things you've been told in the past, or have heard, or even experienced years ago, are much different now in today's church, which has (for the most part) adapted and changed to reflect today's modern society and how we learn and live today.

45

What to Do if You've Never Been to Church

BILL FORTNEY

Don't sweat it. Churches aren't looking for "professional church-goers." In fact, if you've never been to church before, they're going to roll the red carpet out for you, because you are the most coveted person on their radar. They're going to try to have the most impact on someone who's never been before, and they'll be incredibly welcoming. This is especially true because most churches don't really want to steal someone away from another church (well, most don't). Instead, they want to bring in new people—people who need them most. Like you. By the way, here's a great tip if you don't want to stand out as a new church-goer: don't get there early. If the service starts at 10:00 a.m., stroll in around 9:55, just a couple of minutes before it starts, and you'll blend right in. Only the newbies show up early. So, if your goal is to not stand out, then get there with just a few minutes to spare and stroll right on in with the crowd. Also, it's okay to go alone. Churches these days are crazy family-friendly, but you can absolutely go by yourself, and you'll see plenty of others there by themselves, as well. Remember, it's not a dinner party—it's a church service. So, there's no pressure to bring a date, and there's no reason to feel awkward or out of place if you're by yourself. Also, don't worry—you won't be called upon to speak. In church, it's the pastor that does all the talking, so you don't have to worry about being called upon to answer a question, or state your name, or well...anything. They're not going to ask you to stand up and confess your sins or anything crazy like that, so you can relax safe in the knowledge that pastors generally really love to talk and they don't want you cutting into their airtime (I'm kidding about the airtime thing. Kinda).

Christians vs. Denominations

BILL FORTNEY

There's a big difference between being a Christian, and choosing to follow or join a Christian denomination. For example, becoming a Christian means simply that you believe in Jesus (okay, I'm over simplifying it, but that's basically it). However, now that you're a Christian, you might want to choose to join a particular denomination (like choosing to become a Baptist, Catholic, Presbyterian, or Methodist), which is a totally separate thing. Although they are all Christian denominations (and there are many more, like Lutherans, Episcopalians, and Anglicans among others), each one does things in their own way, each has their own set of rules and practices for people who are part of that denomination, and these can vary greatly from denomination to denomination (you can find out a lot about what a church's beliefs and traditions are by visiting their website). You can also choose to be a "non-denominational" Christian, which means you're choosing a Christian church that hasn't officially aligned itself with a particular denomination. So, if you do decide you want to align yourself with a particular denomination, I think the most important thing is to choose one that best fits who you are. If you find a good fit for you, and your life, it makes a big difference towards you enjoying the church and growing there.

What Churches Are Like Today

SCOTT KELBY

When you imagine church, you probably remember it like the church you went to as a kid (providing, of course, you ever went to church in the first place), but because modern society has changed so much, churches have had to change a lot, too. So, don't be surprised if the first church you go to check out is nothing like what you experienced as a kid. Although churches can still be giant cathedrals, they're also in coffee houses, strip malls, or they can meet in someone's home. Wherever they meet, most churches today are very conscious about trying to be relevant, so they try to relate what they're teaching to what's really happening in your life. Chances are, at the very least, you'll think it's interesting, but depending on the church, it might even be fun. Church shouldn't be painful. You should leave feeling great. You should leave feeling energized—pumped up. In fact, you should feel like it's that Sunday that's going to get you through the rest of the week. You should leave feeling like rushing out to find someone less fortunate you can help. Ideally, you should feel some sort of connection to God while you're in church (that's one sure way to know if you've found the right church). However, if you leave feeling bored (or your children leave feeling that way), or sad, or anything other than uplifted, your search for a great church continues.

Tips for Finding a Great Church

BILL FORTNEY

One sure way to find a great church is to ask your friends or co-workers where they go. Chances are good that they did a search to find a great church, and now you can take advantage of their research and give one or more of their churches a try. One of my good friends moved to my area and just did this same thing. He probably visited a dozen or more churches in our area that were recommended to him by people he knew here, and then he settled on one where he really felt comfortable. A few weeks later, he was telling a friend about his new church, and now that friend is going to that same church. Another great way to check out a church is to visit their website (yup, these days almost every church has a website. If they don't have one, don't expect other modern conveniences like running water, air conditioning, or comfortable seats. Kidding. Mostly). Look at their website to learn what they're about, what to wear, what time to be there, and so on. You'll learn a lot there, so take a moment to really check them out. Last but not least, stop in a few and try them out. Nothing beats taking a few for a test drive in person. You'll find out instantly which one best suits you, but again, I'd start by asking friends and looking at church websites first. One more thing: when you think you've found the right one, give it a month. Try it out for a few Sundays and see if it's the one. After a month or so, you'll know.

When You First Walk In

BILL FORTNEY

Believe it or not, churches really want you there. A lot. In fact, many churches these days have people standing in the lobby of the church and their one and only job is to help make sure everyone, especially people new to the church, feel welcome. These people usually got that job because they're incredibly friendly to everyone, and you can usually spot them as soon as you walk in the door (just look for the person with a big smile, shaking everybody's hand as they come in). If it's a smaller church, the pastor may be the one to greet you at the door. Just let the pastor know that it's your first time, and he'll treat you like a long lost friend. He'll show you where to go, he'll probably give you a church bulletin (a program of the day with some announcements) or a brochure about the church, and he'll generally try to make you feel at home because he would love nothing more than for you to come back next Sunday. Don't worry, he won't ask for a donation before you can go in, or anything like that. His job is to make you feel welcome, and asking for money would send most folks right back out the door they just came in. If there isn't someone greeting you at the door, just look for a welcome table, or keep an eye out for a welcome packet—it's for you.

Will They Be Doing Anything Weird?

SCOTT KELBY

Probably (just kidding. I hope). I guess it depends on your definition of weird. For example, you've probably been to a concert and before the concert begins, as you're walking around, you see some wild-looking (and acting) people. You don't leave the concert right then thinking, "Man, this is too weird," because you know that concerts attract all sorts of people. So do churches. When you go to a church for the first time, it's a totally new experience, and each church has its own traditions, and people are sometimes very moved during the service (that "very moved during the service" is my nice way of saying, "they act kinda weird"). I've been to churches where when you least expect it, someone would jump up and yell " Praise the Lord!" That seemed a bit weird to me, but only because nobody ever did that at the church I grew up in (sadly, it kind of cracked me up. Inside anyway). At another church I went to, I saw people raising their hands over their head while the band played music. It seemed a bit weird at first, but once I realized they were just moved by the music, and holding their hands up high helped them connect with God, I was okay with it. I've seen people hold up lighters at concerts and when you think about it, that's probably weirder, but I digress. Anyway, there may be some things that seem a little weird at first, but give it a chance, and ask someone why they're doing it, and it might make total sense. If it doesn't, and you feel uncomfortable, and things get weirder, or someone hands you a snake (kidding), it might be time to find a different church. The bottom line: you shouldn't feel uncomfortable at church. If you do—your search continues.

How Long the Service Lasts

SCOTT KELBY

Every church is different, but they run anywhere from about an hour or so, to in some cases, three hours or more. Of course, you can choose a church whose service is the right length for you, and you can usually find out what time each service is, and how long it lasts on the church's website (like I mentioned, most every church has its own website these days). If it doesn't list how long the service is, and you either want to, or need to leave, you can (it's not prison). In most cases, the restrooms won't be in the same room where the service is held, so you'll see people getting up from time to time, especially if it's a long service. So, if you want to leave, it's okay to get up and quietly go. Don't worry, God won't be mad—He wants you to find a great church, too. Here's another tip for you: when you're trying out a new church, you might want to sit in the back. That way, if you decide to leave, you're just a few short steps from the door.

Bringing the Kids

BILL FORTNEY

If you think your kids will be bored sitting in church with you, you're probably right. That's why even most small churches these days usually have a separate age-appropriate program just for kids (or quiet rooms where you can sit with them during the service). That way, they have fun and are hanging out with kids their own age, they get a church experience that's designed for their age group, and you get one that's designed for you. Check the church's website to find out about their kids' program, which age groups they have programs for, and whether they have a nursery and toddler program (usually all mid-size and larger churches have pretty well-developed kids' programs, and the kids usually love 'em because they mix the learning with fun). Most churches these days are very family-oriented, and they know if your kids love it, you'll probably love it, too, so they go out of their way to make their kids' programs rock. (Just in case you were wondering, most churches these days are very careful about screening workers and creating safe environments for kids.) Also, if you have your kids in the nursery, more and more churches will now give you a beeper, so if the nursery staff needs you (or if your child needs you), they'll just beep you.

If You Were Raised in One Denomination, Are You Stuck There?

BRAD MOORE

Now, if you attended church when you were a child, you probably already have some familiarity with that denomination, but there's probably a reason why you left that church, or you'd still be going there, right? It could be that the church you went to as a child just wasn't a good church (it wasn't well run, the pastor was incredibly boring, etc.), or maybe the pastor just didn't click with you. But, whatever the reason, you're at different place in your life, and now you can choose the type of denomination that actually does fit you and your life as it is now. There is a church out there that's perfect for you, but finding it might take a few visits to other churches. So, I guess the big point here is, don't let the church you went to as a kid be your only reference to what church is all about. A great church can be a blast. You can absolutely love going to church if you do just one single thing—find a great church. They're out there in every community, except Topeka, Kansas (kidding—totally just a joke), and your job is to go out and find one.

Non-Married Couples and Church

BILL FORTNEY

Attending a church service when you're not married is absolutely no problem—you'll see boyfriends and girlfriends of all ages at every service. Now, that being said, not every church will be as excited about having couples that are living together, but are not married. Some churches will welcome you with open arms, and they just want you there no matter what, and others won't be quite as excited. But, I haven't found one yet where you're simply just not welcome (though there are probably a few of them out there for sure, but either way, you won't be asked to provide a marriage certificate when you walk in the door). Also, a lot of churches these days have marriage prep classes, and groups for people who are engaged, and a lot even have what they call "singles' groups," which are especially designed to bring singles in the church together (these singles' groups are a really great place to pick up chicks. Okay, that was wrong. Sorry, I couldn't help myself).

What to Wear and What to Bring

SCOTT KELBY

Every church seems to have their own unwritten dress code. Some want you to dress more formally (suit and tie for men), and some are pretty much "come as you are"— where you'll see people wearing t-shirts, sandals, and shorts. So, what's the dress code for the church you're thinking of checking out? Here's what to do: drive by the church (or pull in the parking lot) on a Sunday morning about 15 minutes before the service is scheduled to begin and simply see what everybody's wearing as they head in. Now you know what to wear. Now, what if you do your "drive by" and the people aren't dressed the way you'd like to dress for church? That's easy—find a different church, one where they dress the way you'll feel most comfortable (after all, I imagine God only cares about what's on the inside anyway). As far as what to bring? Bring money. (Just kidding.) You really don't have to bring anything with you to church. If there's anything you'll need, they'll provide it (but do everybody a favor, and leave your cell phone in the car). For example, churches that ask you to turn to a page in the Bible, will usually have one right there at your seat, so you're not required to bring one of your own. In fact, rather than you bringing stuff, you're more likely to get stuff. They'll probably give you a church bulletin when you first come in, and don't be surprised if after the service the church offers snacks, coffee, refreshments, or in some cases, even full-blown meals. They're very big on members of the church hanging out and visiting with each other (the "church speak" for the act of hanging out with other church-goers and eating yummy food is "fellowship," but that's only because "chillin'" was already taken).

You Don't Have to Sign In or Fill Out Forms

BILL FORTNEY

If you're new to or just visiting a church, there's a 50/50 chance you'll find an information form inside, or along with the church bulletin they hand you when you walk in the door (or that's waiting at every seat when you sit down). This info form is totally optional, and the reason you'd fill it out is if you wanted them to send you more information about the church (maybe you want to talk to somebody about the church in person, or on the phone). But again, only fill out the form if you want the church to contact you in one way or another. I've never heard of a church that requires you to fill out a form or sign-in the first time you walk in the door, but in the unlikely case that this happens, just tell them politely that you'd rather not. If they insist (like a car salesman trying to get you to take a test drive), you've probably picked the wrong church. So, just turn around and head right back out the door. Also, another thing you might possibly run into (though it's happening less and less because people tend to hate this) is that at some point they ask first timer's to stand up. This is an easy one—just don't do it. Don't stand up (but do your best not to snicker at the people that do stand up, because you know and I know they hate having to do that, too). Again, it's probably unlikely this will happen, but at least now you have a game plan in the odd chance that it does.

Running Into People You Know

What happens if you run into someone you know at church—someone who knows your faults, or knows you're not perfect, or just simply knows "you don't go to church?" I've seen this happen more than once, and you know what happens? They're happy to see you (well, most people would be happy to see you, anyway). The further off the track you were, the happier they are that you're there. Church isn't for perfect people. It's not for people who have never done anything wrong. It's for people who want to learn more about God. It's why they're there, and it's why you're there. Now you both have something in common that you didn't have before.

Where to Sit

SCOTT KELBY

There are a lot of folks who have the fear of sitting in a reserved seat at church. Luckily, churches are like Southwest Airlines—you sit wherever you want. So, you don't have to worry about sliding in a row and having someone come up and tell you it's their seat. That doesn't mean people don't have a certain section that they usually like to sit in, but if that section or row is full, people just sit somewhere else (my family always sits on the far-left side of our church. I have no idea why—I think that's where we sat the first time we went, and now that's just where we sit. However, if we get there a little later than usual, and it's full, we just sit somewhere else). So don't feel like you're displacing somebody or sitting in the wrong place—the only wrong place is out in your car. Now, if on the odd chance somebody should come up and tell you you're in their seat (super unlikely, but it could possibly happen), then you'll know right then that you're not only in the wrong seat, you're in the wrong church.

When You're Supposed to Stand or Sit

SCOTT KELBY

Another thing people have some anxiety about is that they'll do the wrong thing at the wrong time (they'll stand when they're supposed to be sitting, or they'll sit when they're supposed to be kneeling, and so on). Churches know that in every service there are some new people there, so that's why the pastor directs the crowd on what to do and when to do it. Luckily, they don't use a secret code. They say things like "Please rise" or "You may be seated," but beyond what the pastor says, just look at the row of people in front of you. If everyone stands up—stand up. It's not a race to see who can stand up the fastest, so if you look around and see everyone starting to stand up, you'll pretty much know what to do (but you don't get extra credit if you spring to your feet like a gazelle). Also, during some services, the pastor will say something, and the audience (called the congregation in church-speak), may respond back in unison. You're not expected to know what to say back, so don't sweat it. Also, don't worry, you won't be required to suddenly yell out "Amen brother!" or "Praise the Lord" or any other spontaneous outburst during the service.

How Loud to Sing

BRAD MOORE

First off, you don't have to sing at all, and you won't be alone. There are people who have been going to church since they were five-years-old and still don't sing. Also, you're not required to belt it out like Aretha Franklin at a stadium concert—you can just sing along at a normal volume. I usually try not to sing louder than the people around me, but there's always one or two people in my general vicinity singing at the top of their lungs, and so far I have never felt compelled to join them in a volume battle. Singing in church is a little different because the songs you sing are actually sung to God and are often referred to as "worship music," and the musicians that play this music are often called a "worship band" or "praise band," so most churches take their music pretty seriously. More formal churches have choirs that sing traditional hymns (most written a couple hundred years ago) accompanied by an organ, and some have modern bands that play the same rock, R&B, jazz, and hip/hop songs you hear on today's Christian radio stations, and some have both. Either way, they want to make sure you have the words, so they'll either project the words to the songs up on a big screen karaoke-style, or they'll have a hymnal (a music book of hymns) at every seat, and they'll tell you which page the hymn is found on. You can sing along or not—it's up to you. But, I will tell you it's usually much more fun if you sing (unless you're standing near me singing really loud).

Putting Money in the Hat

SCOTT KELBY

You knew this was coming, right? Well, here's the scoop: churches pretty much oper-ate on donations from the people who attend that church regularly, and because of that, most churches (but not all), will take up a collection (also sometimes called an offering) during each service. They usually do this by passing around a basket, which people drop money into. As a first time visitor to the church, you're not required, or even expected to make a donation. In fact, you'll never be actually required to do this (after all, it's a donation), but it sure helps the church because it's incredibly expensive to operate a church (and getting more expensive all the time). At the church I attend, right before they pass the basket, the pastor always announces that if this is your first time here, or just visiting, that this one's "on the house," and you don't have to drop anything in the basket. So, in short, when the hat comes around, you can either drop some money in the basket, or just pass it on to the next person. Don't worry—this is a time of very low eye contact from those around you, and nobody's going to give you as much as a furled eyebrow if you pass the basket without dropping something in (especially since there's no way for them to know if you're already making direct dona-tions to the church, or if you're new, or if you're broke). If you don't have any money, or can't make a donation, you could always just drop in a short note thanking them for the service, or just pass the basket right along.

Taking Communion

SCOTT KELBY

Some churches (like all Catholic churches) invite the audience (the congregation) to participate in communion, where you are given a small piece of bread (or a bread-like wafer), and perhaps even a tiny sip of wine (more likely grape juice), as a remembrance of what Jesus did for us by dying on the cross (this ritual was first performed at the Last Supper). You'll notice that not everybody in the church participates, and you absolutely don't have to either. There may come a day when you really want to take part in communion, but don't worry, you won't be expected to, and even if you wind up attending the church for years, it's still not required (which is why not everyone participates). So, if the church you're visiting invites the congregation to communion, you can just sit this one out.

Are They Going to Call Me A Sinner?

BILL FORTNEY

Yup. But they refer to everybody as "a sinner," because we all do things that are considered "sins" (don't worry, they won't single you out. If they did, churches would be very empty). So, you can put that vision of someone standing up, pointing at you, and yelling "You're a sinner!" right out of your mind. Of course, now you might be wondering, "Okay, you say we're all sinners, but what exactly is a sin?" Well, if you asked a group of people "What's a sin?" you'd probably get 10 different answers, though you'd probably hear stuff like, "It's stealing, it's telling a lie, it's being jealous of the things other people have, it's cheating on your spouse, it's killing someone, it's gossiping about your neighbors," etc. Basically, it's doing things God has told us are wrong (and it's stuff you already know is wrong). Now, you might be thinking, "Oh no, I've done some of that stuff just today" (though, hopefully, it's more like "I was jealous of someone today," rather than "I killed someone today"). The thing that makes sin so bad, is that it pushes us farther away from God and the life He wants us to live. Unfortunately, we've all committed so many "sins" in our lives that there's already a gulf between us and God, which is why we need His forgiveness—to put those sins behind us, and build that bridge back to Him. Luckily, to get His forgiveness you only need to ask (more on this later). So, basically, we're all sinners and we're all in this together, so when you hear the term "sinners," it's a generic term for people who aren't perfect (in other words, everybody. Well, except politicians). See that dig I just took at politicians? Is that a sin? Nope, that's a joke. Well, kinda. (Ouch, now that may have just turned into a sin.)

Not Everyone Agrees on Everything

SCOTT KELBY

I talk a lot in this book about certain things being optional, but I want to let you know this up front: there are a lot of different Christian denominations out there, and a lot of different churches with a lot of different ideas about what is right and what is wrong. You will find churches that say it is mandatory that you kneel when praying or God doesn't hear you (I am not kidding), and that having pre-marital sex is a deal breaker, and getting baptized by just being sprinkled with water, and not being fully immersed in it, isn't really being baptized at all (honestly, I am not making this up). I'm not saying they're wrong. They believe it's the right way based on their religious views and how they run their church. So, if you go to a particular church, and they throw you out once they find out you're not married and you're living together (well, they won't actually throw you out, but they'll give that raised-eyebrow look that will make you want to leave), go find a different church. There are plenty that would be thrilled to have you there, just the way you are (which, by the way, would make a great name for a song. "Thriller." You didn't think I was talking about "Just the Way You Are," did you? Wink).

Other Things a Church Can Offer

SCOTT KELBY

Church isn't just about learning about God and Jesus. We've been talking a lot about what you'll learn in church, but it's not unusual for churches today to offer free classes on everything from divorce recovery, to parenting, to financial management, and career counseling (my wife and I took parenting classes from our church that were absolutely invaluable. If we hadn't taken those, I'm sure by now we would probably have sold our kids on eBay). Once you're in a church, you'll be amazed at the range of things they offer that are far beyond just teachings about God, and really worthwhile. Again, you won't know, unless you go (or check their website, but that's kinda cheating).

Now, It's Time for You to Find a Church

SCOTT KELBY

So, now that you know kind of what to expect, it's time to start dating a few churches, and see which one is the right fit for you. Don't marry the first one you check out—try a few different ones in your area and one of those is going to strike a chord with you. There's going to be one where you feel a connection to God, or a connection to the people who go there, or to the pastor, or the music, or something that just lets you know, "This is the one." But you won't really know unless you date a few first. Finding a great church is an important step for you in this journey because it's where you go to learn about God and His plan, and when you find the right church everything else will fall into place. So, when should you start your search? This Sunday.

Chapter Five

Becoming a Christian
Here's What You Need to Do First, Second, and So On

f all the chapters in this book, I imagine this one will be the most surprising to people because after all this, becoming a Christian (which means someone who believes in Jesus Christ) is really easy. Although the act of becoming a Christian (called "accepting Christ") is actually incredibly simple, getting to the point where you have that change inside you where you recognize that you need God's help—that's the hard part, because it requires doing something that many people have a really hard time doing, and that is "having faith." This is all about having faith and trust. At some point, we all have to trust somebody. It's always been that way. Children have to trust their parents, the sick have to trust their doctors, and we all have to trust airline pilots shortly after we quickly move out of the aisles to let others stow away their carry-on luggage. Faith is hard because what people really want in their lives is certainty. We want to know exactly what's going to happen, when it's going to happen, and why. If you think about it, though, accepting Christ actually adds a whole new level of certainty to your life. You may not know what's going to happen next week, next month, or next year, but at least now you'll know what happens after you die. For me, that's a huge thing that gives me a sense of peace, calm, and preparedness that runs through everything I do. So, although you're about to find out that this last little part is really easy, it's that change inside you—where you really gain sincere faith—that's the hard part. If you're there, and you're at a point where you're ready to trust in God to lead you in the right direction, then the good news is you've already done the hard part. So, that makes this more like graduation day—all you have to do is go up and get your diploma, and move on to your new life with new certainty.

Doing a Bunch of Good Deeds Isn't Enough

BILL FORTNEY

If all you had to do were a certain amount of "good deeds" to get into heaven, then it would be easy. You'd do them, mark it off your list, and then go on with your life. Fortunately, that's not how it works. You probably noticed I said "fortunately," because you really don't want it to be a good-deeds thing. Here's why: If you only had to do more good deeds than the guy sitting at the table next to you, then you might be in decent shape, but what if you had to do as many good deeds as Mother Teresa? Then what? (We'd all be in trouble.) Secondly, how many good things would you have do and in what time frame? Would they all have to be really big things? Really bold things? Or could it be just a ton of little good things? And how good is good enough? Is giving $20 to the homeless guy downtown enough, or does it have to be $100. And what if you gave him $100, but you had $400 in your wallet. You could have given him more! Can you see where I'm going with this? Luckily for us, it's much easier than all that (as you'll learn in a moment). Just remember this: doing good deeds might get you a Boy Scout merit badge, but it won't make you a Christian, and it won't get you into heaven. But getting God's forgiveness and accepting Jesus will.

All Your Questions Won't Have to Be Answered First

BILL FORTNEY

When my wife and I were expecting our son (14 years or so ago), we bought just about every book on parenting ever written. We took weeks and weeks of parenting classes, met with other parents, watched videos, and basically totally prepared ourselves for becoming parents. Then we had our baby. We had no idea how many questions we'd have that we never even thought to ask in advance, and we learned more in the first 48 hours of actually having a baby, then we had in literally months of careful study. So, don't expect that you'll have all the answers before you become a Christian, no matter how much you "study up" on Jesus. It's one of those things that you'll just have to experience for yourself, and just like in parenting—no matter how prepared you are in advance—you'll really wind up learning as you go through trial and error. But don't feel alone—hundreds of millions have gone before you using just their faith as their guide, and it worked out wonderfully for them. It'll work for you, too, even if you don't have all the answers (and, of course, as I said in "Nine Things You'll Want to Know... Before Reading This Book!" up front, I don't have all the answers either).

God Had a Plan and We Totally Messed It Up

SCOTT KELBY

Up to this point, we've pretty much spent the whole book talking about God and Jesus, and that He wants the best for us, and so on, but we haven't really talked about how to develop that relationship with God. It helps a lot if you look at what God's original plan for us was, which was to live full, happy lives, and to get along peacefully with one another. Now, how has that worked out? Right. Thousands of years ago, we pretty much rejected God's plan for peace and happiness, and instead of trusting God we decided to do what we wanted to do—lie, cheat, make wars, be greedy, do immoral things, worship all sorts of weird things, and generally mess up so badly, for so long, that God was faced with one of two choices: (1) wipe us out and start all over, or (2) try to save us from ourselves.

He Gave Us a Second Chance

BILL FORTNEY

Luckily, God went with option #2. He loves us (after all, He made us), so instead of wiping us off the face of the earth, He came up with a plan to save us. His plan was to send His Son, Jesus Christ, here to earth to live right along side us. Jesus followed God's plan to the letter to show us that we could live a full, enriching life without all the greed, war, cheating, lying, stealing, and immorality. Jesus was sent here to show us and to teach us how our lives should be lived, and to give us the only way out of the huge mess that we had created for ourselves in the first place. So what is that way out?

Our Way Out of This Mess

SCOTT KELBY

After the first tower collapsed on September 11th, firefighters still poured into the second burning tower because they knew people were trapped and had no way out. They knew, running into that tower, that they might be giving up their lives to save others, but they did it anyway. That is pretty much what Jesus did for us. He literally sacrificed His life for us. We were trapped in this mess we had created, and God's plan to get us out of this mess was to let Jesus die here on earth by being nailed to a cross. With this sacrifice, God put in place a way for us to get forgiveness and start over with a clean slate.

Before You Do This, You Need to Go "All In!"

SCOTT KELBY

If you decided to go on a diet, how successful do you think you'd be if you said, "Well, I'll stay away from most fattening foods, but I'm not going to give up chocolate cake!"? Not very, right? For a diet to work, you have to be "all in"—you have to follow the diet closely and you have to exercise (ugh!). There's no magic pill that lets you eat lots of chocolate cake and french fries, and lose weight (if there was, they could charge $100 a pill, right? Maybe $500). Well, becoming a Christian is kind of the same thing. If you really want all the things I've told you about throughout this book to happen, then you need to be fully committed, you need to go all in (don't you love a book on Jesus that references poker terms?). You can't just say a magic prayer, then go back to doing whatever it was that was tearing your life apart (or the lives of others). You can't just want it. You have to live it. You have to be that compassionate person. You have to help other people. You have to follow the lead of Jesus who showed us that having a fulfilling life comes from living a life of purpose and meaning, not of partying and buying a more expensive TV. Before you turn the page, ask yourself, "Am I all in for this?" Is this what's in your heart? Because if it is, then you're about to take a step that will enrich your life in ways you can't imagine right now. If you're not all in yet, that's okay. Don't turn the page—go back to church. Go to "God school" for a little while longer, because when you're in the place where God is, finding Him becomes much easier. But, if you are ready to turn the page, I'm really proud of you, and really excited for you, too!

Now, First, You Do This

SCOTT KELBY

So here, two thousand and some years later, how do you take God up on His offer? By doing two things: (1) First you have to have faith that Jesus did all this for us—that He gave His life on the cross to help us, and that He proved He was the Son of God by rising again three days after His death. If you take away all the things that man has put into this, like religion and churches, and pastors and televangelists, and all that other stuff, being a Christian really comes down to believing. It's about faith. It's about putting your trust in God, and that His Son sacrificed His life, so you can have a better one.

Then, You Do This

BILL FORTNEY

Over a million people from other countries around the world will become U.S. citizens this year, leaving the country they were born and raised in to make a formal commitment to another country. They've had a change of heart and they've come looking for a new start. They want a better life, a better future, a better place to raise their family, and so on. You're essentially doing the same thing here—you've had a change of heart and you're looking for a new start. You want a better life, and a better future, and so you're making a formal commitment to God. You're going to verbalize what's inside you to God—that you know you're a sinner (good news—you're not alone here), and you're going to ask for His forgiveness for your past sins and then you'll let Him know that in your heart you want to start a fresh new life with Him. So, (2) the next thing you have to do is simply, and sincerely, ask for God's forgiveness.

And Finally This

SCOTT KELBY

Lastly, you need to say a prayer that encompasses those two things we just talked about. This is a sincere act of faith. The exact words you use aren't important. In fact, if you're worried about exactly what words you need to say to get God's forgiveness, you can mark that one off your worry list, because there is not an officially sanctioned phrase, sentence, or paragraph that will do it. It's about your intention. It's about what's in your heart, not which particular words you choose. Whatever you say, if you say it from the heart, you're automatically "in." You don't have to say it out loud—this is between you and God. If you have no idea what to say, and that's stopping you from taking this next step, you can borrow the words of my good friend, Dave Gales. Dave's prayer will work for you, because it's not about the exact words you use to commit yourself to God. Your intention is enough. But, again, if you're stuck, you can pray something along these lines:

God I believe in You, and I realize that I've been in charge of my life and I haven't done such a great job of it, and I need Your help. I know now that You're the only one who can. So please forgive me for what I've done, help me to change, and thank You for sending Your Son Jesus. Amen.

That's it. You don't have to do another step. Can that really be all there is to it? Yes, that's all there is to it. But it's not the end, it's just the beginning.

What's Next? Learning More

BRAD MOORE

This is not a solo sport—you're now a part of a team, so I encourage you to go find a group of other team members to help you along your path in learning about God. Of course, the place you go to learn more about God is (come on, say it with me) church. Besides just learning more about God, you'll learn more about yourself, make new friends and connections, and I'll bet your church probably provides help to people in need. For example, my church feeds the homeless downtown every Saturday, helps migrant workers feed and clothe their kids, they provide food and help for school kids in Haiti, and they helped build an orphanage in Kenya from the ground up. People from our church man all these posts—they're downtown dishing out the food, they're in the fields feeding people, they're in Kenya and Haiti, and wherever else they're needed. You can volunteer to help with causes like these at your church. Helping others is a great way to deepen your connection to God and this helping of others gives both meaning and purpose to your life. Want to learn more? Start at a church. Good news—you get to pick which church.

Learning How to Pray

SCOTT KELBY

Praying is simply talking to God. I do it all the time (though not generally while walking down the street—people start to give me weird looks). I talk to God just like I'm talking to a friend (He is my friend, after all). I talk to Him about anything and everything (not just the big stuff like hopes, dreams, and struggles—I also talk about the deadline I have at work this week, guidance for decisions I need to make, my vacation plans, and the morality to do the right thing instead of the easy thing. You get the idea). I ask God to look out for my family, my friends, and people who I know need His help. I also thank Him for how He has blessed me (trust me, it's a lot more than I deserve). Now, that's just how I pray, but some people prefer a much more formal type of prayer, where you recite a memorized prayer, and that's perfectly fine. How you do it isn't important. What's important is that you're talking to God. What's equally important is that you listen (you probably won't actually hear His voice—if you're hearing voices, we have an entirely different problem). So, when we say "listening to His voice," it's really about listening to that little voice inside you (since God is in you) that says, "You should help these people out," or "You need to take them some food," or "You need to send your 50" HD plasma TV to Scott" (okay, I was taking some liberties with that last one). Those nudges inside you to do good—that's God whispering in your ear (well, your inner ear).

Should You Get Baptized?

BILL FORTNEY

When you get married, you give your spouse a wedding ring as a public symbol of your commitment to each other (okay, it may serve double-duty as it's also a symbol to everybody else that you're taken, but you know what I mean). Well, a baptism is kind of the same thing—it's a public symbol of your love and commitment to God. It's a symbolic washing away of your sins that Christians have been doing since the very beginning, and that's why you're literally dunked in water. In some Christian denominations, you're not required to be baptized (but you may want to anyway as a symbol of your commitment to God, and washing away the past and your mistakes, and starting a fresh new life with Christ). But, in many denominations, it's required to kind of "seal the deal" (so to speak). Sometimes the baptism takes place in a pool. Sometimes a lake. Sometimes an ocean. Sometimes indoors. It just depends on the church. Also, some churches don't dunk you underwater at all—they just sprinkle water on your head. Again, just depends on the church. But, just keep this in mind—it's water. It's not "baptism by battery acid." We get wet all the time, so don't let a little water become a deal breaker for you. I was baptized as a baby by my parents, and then again as an adult. What's the difference (and why twice)? When a baby is baptized, that's a symbol of the parents' commitment to God that the child will be raised as a Christian. When you do it as an adult, this is now your deal—your commitment. It's a very emotional, wonderful, and spiritual event that only takes a minute or two, but its effects last a lifetime. So, should you get baptized? I sure would. (Heck, I did. Twice.)

What is the Bible and Why is It Important?

SCOTT KELBY

The Bible is literally the story of God's love for us, and it's the instruction manual for how we're supposed to live our lives. It pretty much tells us what to do and what not to do. And a lot of it is based on the principle that we need to look out for one another, we need to treat each other with respect, and basically, for the future of this world, we need to literally love one another. It's part guidebook, part love story, and part historical document about what happened here on earth thousands of years ago. It has lessons on everything from how to do business with honesty and integrity to how to raise your children so they grow into good people. One main reason you should read the Bible is because it's another way you'll learn about God. For example, I've written more than 50 books in my career as an author, and if you wanted to learn about me, one place to start would be by reading one of my books. You'd learn about where I'm from, my background, my wife, my kids, my personality, and my quirky sense of humor. Although this is the only book I've ever written about God, you'd have learned by reading my acknowledgments in any one of those other books that I'm a Christian because I always thank God and His Son Jesus Christ. Well, if you want to want to learn about God—read His book. It's the story of His life, His Son's life, and ultimately our lives. It's the must-read book of a lifetime.

Which Bible Should You Read?

BILL FORTNEY

Wait, isn't there just one Bible? Well, yes and no. The one most people think of when they think of the Bible is the *King James Version* (a translation of the Bible from 1611). This is the version that has all the "thou shalts" and "thys" and all the archaic language that for a first-time Bible reader makes it kind of a tough read. Fortunately, there are other options, including translations that are in plain, modern English and that are easy to read, and some of them (like the ones called "study Bibles") will have notes in the margins and other background information, and even maps to help you along the way. The Bible is divided into two sections: The first section is called the "Old Testament," and includes the story of how God created the world and a lot of other stories you've probably heard about (like David and Goliath or Samson and Delilah), but maybe didn't realize were from the Bible. The other section is called the "New Testament," and it's the life story of Jesus and is packed with lessons on how to live our lives. If you were to pick up your first Bible today, I would recommend starting with the New Testament. It's a much easier read and it's considerably shorter. You'll learn about Jesus, and you'll learn the nuts and bolts of the Christian life (and the secret handshake that gets you into heaven. Okay, it's not exactly a handshake *per se*, and it's not a secret, but you'll learn more about Jesus and how to lead a Christian life, so it's worth reading).

Start Forgiving Other People

BILL FORTNEY

Now that you've been forgiven, do one of the best things you can do for yourself—forgive people who have wronged you. I'm not saying you have to forget what they've done and pretend it never happened, but forgive them. Totally. Let it go. Put the incident behind you and let it go. This is one of the best things I've ever done and I am such a happier person for it. Now, you might be thinking, "They don't deserve my forgiveness!" That may be true, but just remember, doing this is not for them. It's for you. Letting that hurt you have inside finally go, will help heal you in a way no other can. Look back at the people who have wronged you, who mistreated you, and took advantage of you, and then simply forgive them. They're human. They messed up. Don't compound their mistake by making it your own. This has more power than you'd think. Do it today and then it's done. But just remember to be ready to forgive in the future, also. Sadly, those aren't the last people who'll do you wrong in this life.

Tell Someone You Accepted Christ

BILL FORTNEY

Whenever something important happens in our lives, what's the first thing we do? We tell all our friends, family, co-workers—you name it. Even if it's just something fun, like you saw a really cool movie, or ate in a really great restaurant, or your kid does something great at school or in sports, the first thing you do is tell someone about it. This is the same thing. When you tell someone that you've become a Christian, it will help make it more real to you, and to the people around you (by the way, you don't need to go stopping strangers on the street—you'll just weird them out). Anyway, it may sound silly until you actually do it, but it kind of seals the deal (not with God—you're already good with Him, but within yourself).

Chapter Six

What to Expect Next
What Life is Like After Becoming a Christian

I f you're reading this chapter, let me be the first to congratulate you (although you know and I know you've probably already told a dozen people, but for the sake of this chapter intro let's just pretend I'm the first). I hope you take a moment to really soak in the fact that all that junk from your past is behind you, and that you're starting fresh, totally forgiven, and ready to walk through life knowing that you're not alone. Now, I don't do this a whole lot in the book, but I want to give you some personal advice moving forward: God has totally forgiven you and put every bad thing, every lie, and everything you're embarrassed about behind you. Now, you have to let it go. All of it. It's truly behind you, and it's not a part of the new you. Focusing on that old stuff—even talking about it—won't help you in any way. Avoiding that stuff will. You've been dealt a new hand. A fresh life. Few people ever get the opportunity to wash the past away, but you just did. Now, you probably have some expectations of how life will be from now on, and some of them may be right on the money, and some of them (things you now expect from God), might be...well...you just need to read this chapter, so you keep things in perspective. Remember, you didn't become a Christian to get a bunch of stuff. You became a Christian to give a bunch a stuff. Your transformation to this point might have been quick, or it might have a been a long and winding road, but just remember, at this point, where you've just accepted Christ, the journey has just begun (insert dramatic music here).

God's Not Going to Solve All Your Problems

BILL FORTNEY

Just because you've become a Christian, don't expect God to suddenly wave a magic wand over you, and all your problems disappear (because He actually waves a golden chalice instead. Kidding!). Christians have problems just like everybody else, but at least now you're forgiven and starting with a clean slate, and more importantly— you're no longer "going it alone." Just knowing that you're not alone in life and no longer empty inside makes dealing with the daily problems of life that much easier. It changes your attitude about dealing with problems, and my guess is that you'll be listening to that inner voice more than before and it'll help steer you in the right direction, if you'll just listen. If you find a church, then you'll have people who genuinely care about you, will help you deal with your struggles, and you'll learn to never underestimate the power of prayer in tough situations. Plus, although I may never meet you in person, I'm on your side, too (after all, I wrote this book for you). Anyway, I just wanted you to know that, although your problems won't magically disappear, just knowing you're not alone does change your attitude and outlook, and those two things are powerful allies in dealing with the stuff life throws at us.

Bad Things Can and Will Still Happen

BILL FORTNEY

Being a Christian doesn't put an impenetrable force field around you that shields you from bad things—if it did, there would be no need for this book, because that's a pretty strong selling point. Also, being a Christian isn't a detour around life's problems. In fact, God expects you to do your part to avoid bad things. For example, if your doctor warns you that you're in danger of becoming a diabetic, you have to change your eating habits. You can't just keep eating high-sugar and high-carbohydrate foods, and then ask God to keep your blood sugar at normal levels. It just doesn't work that way. But here's the deal: your new relationship with God is a foundation that helps you get through the toughest stuff life throws at you and helps you come out the other side in one piece. How many times have you heard stories of people who endured horrible situations and they said "It was my faith in God that got me through, and gave me hope that one day I'd be free." What happens to the people who don't have that faith? How do they deal with life's deepest darkest days? Honestly, I have no idea. I could never endure such times of deep despair alone. The good news is now you don't have to either. But, at the end of the day, remember this: you didn't decide to become a Christian because of the benefits plan (well, eternal benefits aside), you probably did it because something was missing inside you—something that would give your life meaning, hope, and a new beginning—and now that you've found God, you may not have an outer force field, but you certainly now have an inner one.

Be Patient with Yourself and with God

BILL FORTNEY

Okay, so you've accepted Christ, you're a Christian, but you're still making the same mistakes, getting tripped up by the same things, and you're wondering where God is. Isn't He supposed to swoop in and fix everything? Well…not exactly. First, be patient. Be patient with yourself and be patient with God. It's not like you signed up for the military and the next day you've got a buzz cut and you're wearing fatigues. This is a gradual transformation, so be patient with yourself. You know that helping others is a part of what you should do, but you don't have to rush out the next day and start feeding the homeless. Opportunities to provide help, relief, hope, and kindness will appear, but they might not appear this afternoon. Luckily, I think now you'll be much more aware of those opportunities—ones you might have missed or totally overlooked before. Also, cut yourself some slack. Give yourself some time to adjust to the "new you." It'll happen, but it's more like a butterfly's metamorphosis than just flipping a light switch. This is a life style—not a New Year's resolution. If you find yourself making mistakes, just remember—you're the new guy. You're a newbie (or what my son would call "a noob") and you'll get it. If you make a mistake, don't beat yourself to death over it. The fact that you're concerned about it at all just shows you're making progress.

How God Lives Inside You

SCOTT KELBY

In a number of places in the book (and in one of the chapters about God on the book's companion website), I mention that God is inside you, and I totally believe that's true (versus God that looks down upon us from a giant cloud in the sky). That concept really hit home with me when 11 years ago I took a trip to China with my brother and father (it was always my dad's dream to see China), and the first night we were there I got down on my knees to say my prayers before bed (by the way, the knees thing is totally optional—it won't get you in or keep you out of heaven). I was literally halfway around the world in a place I'd never been, but as soon as I started to say my prayers I felt exactly the same closeness to God as if I was in my bedroom at home. At that moment I realized that the reason was because God is in me. He was there with me. No matter where I go, no matter what I do, He is always right there. When you hear Christians talk about never being alone, this is one of the things they're talking about. God is with you every step of the way.

Your Closeness to God Can Go Up and Down

SCOTT KELBY

Right now, you probably feel closer to God than you ever thought possible, but just remember that your relationship with God is like any other relationship—it takes a little work to keep it healthy and growing. For example, what do you have to do to kill a house plant? You don't have to rip it out by the roots or take a Weed Wacker to it. All you have to actually do is just do nothing. Don't water it. Don't nurture it. And don't worry—it'll die. The same thing with your marriage. Do nothing and it will die. You don't have to have a huge fight or have an affair—it'll eventually die on its own if you don't do some work to keep it healthy. The same thing holds true of your relationship with God. To warm things up, do something that brings you closer to God. Talk to Him. Often. Just like the best marriages are the ones where the couple communicates. Same with God. Talk to Him. Read a historical document about Him and His Son's life here on earth (the Bible). Spend time with Him. Spend time with other people who know God. Go to places where God hangs out or help other people less fortunate than you, and He'll be there with you. Put a little work into your relationship and I promise you, you'll stay connected.

It's Okay to Enjoy Life

SCOTT KELBY

So much is written about the great things that will happen to you after you leave this earth, but I believe God wants you to have fun, laugh a lot, and enjoy the life He's given you here on earth. Look at the amazing natural wonders He's given us (ever watch a sunrise at Utah's Monument Valley, or a sunset along California's Pacific Coast Highway? Unreal!). Look at the majestic mountains, amazing animals, listen to beautiful music, taste delicious foods—He put them all here for us to enjoy. Also, it's okay to like nice things—everybody likes nice things, but now you have another layer of things that make you happy that isn't just "stuff." So, laugh a lot, eat amazing foods, and travel to fascinating places, but remember—these are all gifts. Be thankful for them. Always.

Your Priorities Will Change

SCOTT KELBY

Now that you're a Christian, your priorities are going to change. It's kind of like when you first have kids. When you're a married couple without kids, all you have to worry about is where you're going to dinner, which club you're going to after dinner, and which movie you're going to catch on Saturday night. Then you have kids and suddenly your priorities change. Now you're concerned about finding the safest car seat, and if the baby food you're buying is organic, and which diapers are the most comfortable for your baby. This all happens automatically. You didn't sit down and say, "We need to change our priorities." It just happens, and the things that made you happy before (dinner, dancing, movies) get replaced by wanting to play with your baby, and just lying there watching her play with her baby toys, and making darn sure you're there for her first steps. The weird thing is—you give up all that other stuff without even thinking, because something so much more meaningful has come along that it makes choosing a restaurant or nightclub seem silly in comparison. The same thing kind of happens when you become a Christian. Now, getting the latest cell phone isn't the driving force in your life, but making sure the food bank gets their delivery Saturday morning somehow becomes very important to you. Plus, you can always get that cell phone on your way back from helping at the orphanage. ;-)

God Answers All Prayers (But Sometimes His Answer is "No")

BRAD MOORE

I remember as a young man being heartbroken when a girl I had been dating broke up with me. I remember praying to God, "Help me find a way to get her back." God heard my prayer, but His answer was "No." Looking back on it, God was 100% right because had we gotten married (a) it would have been a total unmitigated disaster (I can see that now but, of course, I couldn't at the time), and (b) I never would have met the woman of my dreams, whom thankfully I did marry (22 years ago), and today we have two amazing kids and a life filled with love. God has a plan for each of us. His plan wasn't for me to ruin my life by marrying the wrong woman. He had a different plan for me in mind, and that's why He said, "No" (thanks God!). Now, look back on your own life—on people you might have married, or business deals you might have entered into, or things you might have done that would have impacted your life in really nega- tive ways that seem so clear now, but you couldn't see it at the time because you were too emotionally involved in the decision. I know God heard my prayer, and although I wasn't happy with His answer at the time, now I totally "get it." When I was a little boy, and my parents warned me not to stick a fork into an electrical socket, I didn't fully un- derstand why, but I trusted that they were looking out for me, so I didn't do it. It's the same with God. Even when I don't know why He's saying, "No," I trust that He's looking out for me. He knows things I just don't.

Pastors Are Human After All

SCOTT KELBY

When someone decides to become a pastor, it's definitely a calling from God—something inside them tells them this is what they're supposed to do (just like some people are called to be firefighters, police officers, or join the military). No-body does it because it's a cushy job—ask any priest, pastor, or minister. However, just because they have an inner calling to help people and to teach people doesn't mean they're "super people." They're human just like you and me, and they mess up just like you and me. The problem is the spotlight is on them, so their mistakes and mess ups are much more visible (believe me, you wouldn't want to live your daily life with that spotlight of "you're supposed to be better than us" shining on you 24/7). Anyway, just like there are medical doctors that smoke cigarettes, financial consultants that have to declare bankruptcy, and police officers that break the law, you'll find there are pastors and ministers that mess up, too, and give into life's urges and desires just like the rest of us. Now, in the end, God may judge them more harshly than He does us, because He called them to do His work, but that's not our job—judging them. Our job is forgiving them, and understanding that they're not a higher life form sent here from another planet. They're human.

Some People Use This For Business Reasons

You probably already knew this, but some people see church as an opportunity for business networking, so don't be surprised if somebody hands you a business card and on that card it mentions they're "a Christian business." Now, why would someone put their religious affiliation on their business card? To get more business. It kind of implies that, "It's okay to buy from me. I'm a Christian. I'll give you a better deal than other people or I won't rip you off like the other guy" (and things along those lines). Just so you know, if their business card says "a Christian business," that doesn't necessarily mean it's a good business or that they'll give you a better deal than the next guy. It just means they don't mind using their Christianity as a marketing tool to get more business. But it doesn't just stop in business. Some politicians have used this ploy for years (just look at their campaign ads on TV with them carrying a Bible on their way out of church). Anyway, not everyone that lets you know they run a Christian business is a bad person or an unethical businessman, and not every politician who says they are a Christian is disingenuous. I'm just letting you know it's something to keep an eye out for.

You Don't Have to Stop Hanging Out with Non-Christians

BRAD MOORE

Don't worry—now that you're a Christian, you don't have to cut ties with your non-Christian friends. I have lots of friends who aren't Christian (maybe God wants me to hang out with them, so they have contact with a Christian). Instead, just sit back and take a look at the people who are your friends and ask yourself if you're hanging out with good, quality people. People who genuinely want the best for you. People who build you up (not tear you down). My friend Douglas says, "Show me who they hang out with, and I'll show you their future." He's right. If they hang out with criminals, it won't be that long before they get in trouble. If they hang out with people who drink, they'll be drinking soon, too. The people you spend time with greatly influence you and your entire life (that's why parents are so concerned about who their kids hang out with), so just make darn sure you're hanging out with good, quality people. They are a mirror of your future.

You Don't Have to Start Converting Others

BILL FORTNEY

As I've mentioned, this isn't a multi-level marketing scheme, so you don't have to rush out and get 12 other people to sign on. Don't send one of those "I am now holier-than-thou" emails out to all the people in your email list. Don't start preaching to your friends and calling them out for their mistakes, etc. Just let your actions speak for you now. One of the cornerstones of being a Christian is helping others through acts of charity. Once other people see you doing these things, honestly, that's enough. When people see the change in you, odds are they'll want to know what happened. I'm guessing that one day they'll ask, and if they're asking questions, that's an opportune time to talk with them about what Jesus has done in your life, and what He could do in theirs (of course, if you decided to send them a copy of this book, too, that wouldn't hurt my feelings one bit. Hint, hint).

You'll Meet Other Christians Who Are...Well... Not Exactly Walking-the-Walk

SCOTT KELBY

Now and then, you're going to run into Christians who don't fit the mold of what you think a Christian should be, or how a Christian should act. We're all a work in progress, so don't be surprised when you run into someone who says they're a Christian doing some very un-Christian-like things. When you see this happening, cut them some slack. We've all got our stuff. We're all a work in progress, and we all struggle from time to time with doing the right thing. Don't shun these people, but be there to help them if they ask for it. Just remember, change doesn't happen overnight—it happens over time. For them, and for you.

You'll Meet Other Christians Who Think They Know Exactly How You Should Walk–the–Walk

BILL FORTNEY

Even though, technically, Christians are not supposed to judge others, don't be surprised if you run into a Christian or two who, upon learning that you are now a Christian, feel that it's their job to now tell you "the rules" as they see them. For example, you might run into a Christian who tells you, "Well, now that you're a Christian, you can't see this movie or that movie, and you have to vote for this politician or that one, and you can't have an alcoholic drink," and so on. They'll basically try and take the way *they* (or the particular Christian domination they chose) feel about these things and try to transfer them onto you. This isn't God's plan for you. This is their plan for you, and of course, they interpret their plan as "God's plan." So, don't let it freak you out when someone starts spouting off "the rules to being a Christian" to you. Remember, it's not *"the* rules." It's *"their* rules." God has a custom-made plan for you, and it may be very different than His plan for them. So, just ask yourself if what you're hearing is what God wants you to do, or is this what your co-worker, neighbor, or friend thinks you should do.

Share This Book with Five Other People or in 10 Days a Terrible Plague Will Rain Upon You

SCOTT KELBY

Okay, that's not entirely true (it will happen in just eight days, and it won't actually be a plague—it'll be more like a runny nose and maybe a bit of a cough). I am hoping that this book has changed you, moved you, challenged you, made you think, and made you pray to the point that you took that leap of faith and accepted Christ. My sincere hope is that if you started this book as a "wanna be-liever," as you read this, now you're a Christian with a new clean slate and a fascinating life ahead. If that's the case, I hope you'll go one step further and hand another "wanna be-liever" in your life this book. You'll be giving them a chance to receive a gift that can change their life here on earth, and beyond, in a very significant way. Maybe this will be the one book that reaches them. Maybe this will be the book that provides that little spark, that lights that flame, that winds up filling in that empty space inside them where God is supposed to live. Maybe one day someone will thank you for caring enough to go that one step further for them. Maybe you'll be responsible for one more person on this planet who be-comes dedicated to helping others, who becomes part of the hope and part of the so-lution for this world at a time where we really need people to care about one another, to help one another, and to put others before themselves. What do you have to lose, knowing what they have to gain? So, pass this book on to some folks who could use it. Maybe it was actually written just for them. Hey, ya never know.